Testament:
A Rural Anthology

Book Two in The Rural Anthology Series
by Backwoods Literary Press

Editor-in-Chief - Belle Townsend

Managing Editor - Trish J. Gibson

Supporting Editors - Shiloh Stump,
Olivia Dudding-Rodriguez, Bayley Hope Amburgey,
and Samantha Ratcliffe

Foreword by Surabhi Balachander

Cover Art by Ceirra Evans

Backwoods Literary Press
A non-profit project fiscally sponsored by the
Appalachian Community Fund
backwoodsliterarypress.com

Identifier:
ISBN 979-8-218-94288-5

Testament:
A Rural Anthology

Book Two in The Rural Anthology Series
by Backwoods Literary Press

Table of Contents

Foreword: Cicada Ethics *by Surabhi Balachander*

As soon as I heard about *Discarded: A Rural Anthology* (2024), Backwoods Literary Press's first publication, I rushed to read it. I am a professor of American literature, and for the past decade, I've been working on projects about rural identity in American literature from 1920 to 2020, the first century during which, at least by the metrics of the U.S. Census, "rural" was a minority position in the U.S. Like most people with an attachment to or investment in rural America, I've long been tired of urban media narratives that reduce a large, diverse portion of the country to its supposed role in electoral politics. As Bradley Firchow says in his piece in *Testament*, "What they know about this place is often what made the news. // And what made the news barely eclipses the truth." In my book-in-progress, I constellate a lot of different literary works to illustrate that rural America is multiethnic and cosmopolitan. Reading *Discarded*, I thought, here it all is, in one anthology. Of course no single collection can really represent everything about rural America, but *Discarded* brought together a diverse range of contributors, showcased complex attachments to place and negotiations of rural identity, was unapologetically queer and rooted in a strong sense of justice. I loved it. Since I finished reading it, I've kept *Discarded* on my desk so that I can glance at or flip through it as I work. It was an honor to be invited to write the foreword for *Testament*, which continues this important project.

Testament's center of gravity is in Kentucky, owing largely to the community-based spirit of the Kentuckians who made it happen. Looking through the author bios, you can discern community networks and regional connections among many of these writers. The entire project of Backwoods Literary Press is to encourage and platform rural-identified writers who may or may not have formal creative writing training, but who all really have something to say. The press even held a series of generative writing workshops before releasing the call for submissions, one of which I was lucky enough to attend. While Kentucky takes up the most space, this anthology also represents writers from thirty states across the South and Appalachia, the Midwest, and other regions.

Reading this book is reading place. For most of these writers, and, I would venture, for most rural people, rural identity derives from a deep connection to place. They think about what makes a place home, how their bodies and communities move through the landscape. Em Shepardson, breaking down the human/environment binary, describes their trans body as "a map of the Midwest." Amy Le Ann Richardson recounts learning to read the sky and asserts, "The land doesn't forget who listens," a sentiment Mecca Collins echoes: "when I hear the creeks speak … I listen." People and place are very much in complicated, emotional, reciprocal relationship in the pieces collected here. Lexie Stepro writes of a journey home, "I … drive the backroads like I'm forgiving them. / I'm hoping they'll forgive me too."

There's a biblical association with "testament," of course, and many writers featured here wrestle with Christianity, both chafing against certain manifestations of it and finding meaning in faith. The poems, both declarative and associative in their modes, do testify. The title also calls up "last will and testament," suggesting inheritance, a theme that comes up repeatedly across these pieces. There's familial lineage in home places. Ellen Pauley Goff writes of trying on a grandmother's farm dress, Emily Crenshaw of a grandmother's ring. In other places, this inheritance is expansive, forward-looking—Marjorie Maddox writes, "what you become you pass on." And there's a grief contained within inheritance—to inherit something is, often, to carry it into a new generation as an older one fades. Death and decay, grief and loss, run through this anthology. Poets mourn ancestors, friends, ways of life. Grief can be consuming, animating, as for Ja'Quacy Kieron Minter: "What is nostalgia, if not grief? What is grief if not a boy burning from the inside out?" And it can also be a backdrop for something greater—from Kelsey Voit, "Amidst death and dance, / I burst into joy, / witness to gratitude."

There's a rootedness that characterizes the pieces here, whether the writers come from generations of people who made their home in the same place or from recent migrants or immigrants. Roots venture underground into the soil, communicate with microbes, form networks, take hold. "My love is thick roots running through tight soil—grounded," Thailan Franklin writes. There's a lot of activity underground across the anthology, actually, from planting seeds to unearthing skulls. These writers show a commitment to not just looking, but listening, feeling, being beneath the surface.

As I read through the pieces collected here, I was struck by a particular underground image: cicadas. Eight pieces by different writers mention them. Periodical cicadas live underground as nymphs for thirteen or seventeen years, and then, all of a sudden, all together, emerge on the surface, filling rural spaces with their cacophonous grating. As a Midwesterner, I have my fair share of cicada memories. I remember the last emergence of the legendary Brood X, in the spring and summer of 2021. I lived in Michigan then. Newly vaccinated against COVID-19, my friends and I were also emerging from a deep pandemic winter, cautiously gathering again. One friend shared regular updates on the status of Brood X alongside his memories of their last emergence, when he was a teenager in Ohio. When he excitedly said, "The cicadas are coming!" I felt him honoring a past version of himself.

In 2021, the cicadas were not subtle. We heard them constantly, avoided stepping on them on walks. They flew into a car and caused a crash, swarmed a plane's engines and delayed the president's press corps. Eventually, we saw their spent corpses pile up. The next generation of Brood X will not emerge until 2038; I wonder which pasts we will honor, which futures we will imagine, then. Being underground can be a temporary state. Things move in cycles, even if we can't always see the patterns while we're in them. Idris Isaiah Irihamye writes, "I want to believe there is a voice / louder than a nation's intent to kill." There's a cicada ethic to this anthology, I think. As you read the pieces in *Testament*, I invite you to think about what kinds of exuberant, disruptive, collective emergence they represent. Listen for the noise.

Surabhi Balachander

Corvallis, Oregon

October 2025

A Letter from the Editor: Holding What's Here
by Belle Townsend

I've been thinking about the marks we make. The lines drawn on maps that decide who gets clean water and who doesn't. The policies written in distant rooms that reshape communities, funneling power to a few while taking it from the many. The marks that define borders, land deeds, entire histories—and the distortions that shape them just as much. You see, erasure isn't about forgetting. It's about engineering. It's the deliberate shaping of narratives: who gets heard, who gets documented, who is left out entirely. And it's in those gaps that the truths of our lives are buried.

In the big picture, some rural places are written off as cautionary tales. Others are flattened into nostalgia, sentimentalized into idyllic nuclear family postcards, or dismissed as empty flyover zones. The reality—of land, of labor, of us—gets buried under headlines, propaganda, and the endless chatter of outsiders claiming to understand what they've never touched, tilled, or tasted. These places aren't "backwards." They're living, breathing, layered, complicated, ours. Narratives spun on screens, in print, or even plastered along the highway are engineered to divide and control: to pit us against each other in our own towns, and to turn the rest of the country against us, too. And yes, it works, because they've trained us to doubt each other while the real architects of extraction keep their hands on the levers. *Testament* is a direct response to all the ways our stories get erased and misrepresented. It's proof that, even when we're on different corners fussing over the specifics of this or that, we share the same fight.

This anthology series began like most sacred things do: a porch light flickering above a late-night smoke, a call stretching past cell service into static, a back booth at the only place still open. From these small sparks, voices began to gather, to reach beyond fostered isolation. What you hold in your hands isn't a tidy record or a single perspective. This is a collective offering, a refusal, a gathering shaped by lineage, survival, memory, faith, and fire. Inside, you'll find poems that reach like prayers, essays that don't flinch, and truths pressing against every attempt to contain them.

These pieces aren't just about what's been discarded; they're declarations of what endures—land that holds us, neighbors who show up when it counts, grief that has lingered long enough to find its shape, and people who carry weight yet still open their palms to offer something to you, to us. But you're not just invited to read this. You're invited to take what resonates and hold it with care. Let it shape you. Let it stir something, because documenting like this doesn't just preserve what was. It resists the kind of erasure that excludes people from the record, where power rewrites history to tighten its grip on what comes next. These stories carry the lessons of us and those who came before us: how they were harmed, how they fought back, and what they made possible. And in telling the fuller story, they crack open what we believe all of this can look like. The narratives we inherit shape the paths we're told we can, or cannot, follow, and by reclaiming them, we begin to name a future on our own terms.

These pieces speak to more than individual memory; they point toward collective power. In gathering these testaments, we're not just archiving what's been; we're reminding ourselves that history is a living thing, and we can shape it. Some of us do that through art. Some through organizing. Some through kitchen-table conversations, collective bargaining, or casserole drop-offs. These are all ways we resist fostered isolation. These are all ways we say: *we matter to each other, even through all the bullshit.* Imagine how many dollars were spent, how many consultants were hired, how many pages of Project 2025 were dedicated to censoring stories like the ones in this book. And now, imagine how little it matters, because we found each other anyway; and we'll keep finding each other, no matter what. We win in every iteration of this archetype, and I am honored to stand with you here, in the middle, where we get to decide how many chapters we'll let be written for us.

Another world is always taking root, sometimes right under our feet. Creation, in the face of erasure, is a way forward—to name ourselves, mark the map in our own handwriting, and say: we were here, we are here, and there's no way in hell we're done yet.

With love,
Belle

Please, take care while reading.

This book contains mentions of drug use, alcohol, addiction, sex, intimate partner violence, physical violence, blood, vomit, death, pet and animal death, murder, homophobia, transphobia, racism, and some themes that may be considered adult or mature.

Carpenter Cemetery *by Makayla Danielle Gay*

We're going
on up
the hill

        singing with
         the hill

                sleeping with
                 the hill.

We approached death with full plates.
Once the cicadas fell
from their slick resin,
we drove Cheverlets full
up to the hill.

Us kids squatted out of sight
to pluck legs off daddy longs
till the preaching and tinny singing
stopped and we answered by
tearing free, screaming—wild
like the banshees, our family left back
on a further hill.

I've never used to think of death or dying.
I only thought of biscuits still warm
in their tins and smiling in pretty dresses
next to cousins who didn't have to climb up
the hill this year.

*Previously published in Appalachian Review in their
Fall 2023 issue, and later collected in Hackles, Girl
Noise Press (2025).*

Justification *by Cassandra Ruby*

The white man watches me pay for my groceries.
Conforming back into the Anglo-Saxon,
caught his eyes surprised that
it wasn't an EBT. He smiled.
I smiled back.
Trump is president.
I am the daughter of Maliche,
assimilating into the melting pot,
translating for the enemy,
and I just started the justification process,
overlooking the whispers of my ancestors.
They'll kill you too.
An egg floats
in a cup,
next to my bed.
President of America
gave me ojo.

The Worlds of Tomorrow *by Idris Isaiah Irihamye*

I believe freedom is a void you sing into,
or maybe it is the song.
I believe hope is the end of the sentence
when everything you meant is no longer possible,
but what has been said is finally finished.

I lived my life wanting to believe
that there was no more evil to be done,
that we had grown full and nauseous on our violence
and if we could just breathe,
if we could just understand,
we could make the pain stop.

I don't know what to believe in anymore.
I gave my blood to a goddess of justice
      and my heart to a martyr, but
           my body is iron and sand;
              my poems are spit and wind;
         and not bread,
      and not papers,
and not their youngest daughter back.

I want to believe that there are protons
resisting, flickering in the oblivion,
just the smallest things.
Though they are smaller
than the baby's fingers, smaller
than a torn veil,
and do not make up for anything.

I want to believe there is a voice
louder than a nation's intent to kill.
I want to believe that the people and their soft hands,
their warm jaws, their magnetic eyes,
that their God knows their prayers.

I want to believe that humanity amounts to something
beautiful, that they make us amount
to something beautiful.

I want to believe that we can be saved,
but I don't want to have to believe in saviors
anymore. I want to just believe. I want, I want,

I want to believe that there are fields of olive trees,
and knafeh dripping simple syrup
in the Worlds of their Tomorrows.
I want to believe that young boys fish until dusk
in Lake Kivu and women laugh
until they topple from their braiding chairs.
I want to believe that the night goddess-sky over Juba
and Khartoum winks in pleasure and music drifts
over the savanna and fills the streets.
I want to believe that a feathered serpent sleeps,
in peace, in the hearts of his people and a drum beat
heats the floor under their feet.

I believe our people have love enough
        to make our worlds beautiful
                again. We just want tomorrow
        to be beautiful.
We just want it to sing.

'Til Every Battle's Won *by Noah Edgar*

*In August 1974, Lawrence Jones, a 23-year-old miner
striking in Harlan County, Kentucky, was fatally shot by
a company foreman, Billy C. Bruner, during the
Brookside coal mine strike, sparking a massive upsurge
in militancy and ultimately leading to a contract with the
UMWA.*

Neared the end of our rope   peelin' back scabs   picked
our bodies thin   and scraped to a fine resin.

Brutal! By God   we was flammable
as a Friday night, and the picket line was a'fixin'

fer a party.   Women was buckled to asphalt   pluckin'
they ribs   like geetar strings   cryin' out   our voices
gathered to a tune:

Which side are you on
Which side are you on

Cause there are no neutrals   no meet me halfway's
Only a pressure to protect   pride   material

peace. I heard this in the union hall. I heard it in song.
And we was so young
Lawrence and I side by side   grippin' bottlenecks of
empty Millers   flashin' pistols for show

a fight loomin' over like the winged shadow
of a vulture   darknin' over a corpse on the road.

There'd been talk of histories   machine guns
blood and battle. I wondered   why work

if my weapon is just a lack   of labor
if my body is not a body   but a bridge

to a better future?   and if the blood is still
warm   then why push for peace?

But when Billy Bruner came fumblin' in
all hostile   a shotgun pressed to his hip

there wasn't no time to think   just Lawrence
and Bruner shootin' words at each other

the blood rushin' to they faces   then
like a forest on fire   smoke fumin'

and a ringin' pingin' from ear to ear.
I took my pistol from my pocket   fired

till I heard a click.   The cracks of bullets died
down   then a weight over my shoulder

it was Lawrence   his head   hallowed in the back.
Blood and brains   warm on the picket line.

Backwater Hymn by *Ellen Pauley Goff*

I wear your farm dress in the hot August dusk
is how I begin the letter to my grandmother.
When you were young, you must have prayed
for a new horizon, that city sound, I think
as I exhume this delicate thing slip you wore
before motherhood took shape.
You told me our mountains echo
with a heartbeat of mayhem, a hymn
of power and promise for hungry girls,
so listen and hush as the womenfolk bestow
this wisdom, a rhythmic remedy to a one-note
cage. I'm trying now to escape but these hills
they still thrum with threat, and caution
Be Good and Don't Stray too far from the path
of the righteous and the gospel of the honest girl
for she is the sun at the center of their lore.
These sermons never age, no sir, but they
sure as hell get old real quick, we're all stuck
in the same backwater myth.
Even a sun burns out at some point
if it can't breathe. So how do we grow
when our mountain is hollow, cored empty,
earth-worm-tracks-through-a-crab-apple
rotten. Is this how you felt at my age,
boiling from the inside out?
This dress doesn't hug but hangs loose,
forgiving, shielding my edges. So I think
this must be how you survived
the summers, when these hills howled
with heat, the body a balloon of humidity
full as rain clouds, swollen heavier than
history, thicker than lard.
Lord above, us girls bellow to the heavens,
Can we for one day, one hour, one second not

be touched? What could we have climbed
all these centuries had we been allowed
to properly breathe? You have no idea
the gift you've left behind, me
your granddaughter, with this old rag
you wore to look pretty once upon a time.
All this to say, thank you for the cloth cut,
the anger demanded to be a woman
unseen. I promise to remember this when
I wear your farm dress in the hot August dusk.

Gibbet *or* Learning to be Queer in This Place
by Melissa Helton

At the end of the driveway hangs an empty gibbet,
too heavy for even the wildest gale to budge.
No rotting corpse. No skeletal pile. Just the patient
threat I can be hung out as a warning.
Just the quiet iron reminder that their mercy
is all that keeps me from it, the empty cage
as eager to be filled as a rumbling stomach,
as the children's neon easter baskets.

Even the Locusts *by Leigh Claire Schmidli*
for Gran

In our shared bed,
snoring, she'd wake me.
Her hair, April-gray curls
heaped atop the pillow, curls
that held on, always,
and all through the night.
I crawled from the bed, calling on Ma
to nudge her that certain way.
And the noise would stop.
She never remembered the nudges, though—
her sleep unbroken—
'til morning, and Ma told her
the number.

Bless 'er heart, she'd say.
My heart.

Shuffling cards with her elbow-like thumb
that could not unbend, she'd talk about
the cousins, the corn,
the folded laundry, and the locusts.
Shuffling the stories in her deck—playing
the same ones. And we always remembered
the ones from before.
I still looked at her, pretending I didn't notice
the repetition,
as if I were letting a child play the wrong card—
a heart atop a diamond—
to keep the game going.
Others had a habit of leaving her
to her own voice.
But I didn't mind what she said.
She was talking; she was talking to us all.

Bless 'er heart.
The cousins' hearts, the farmers' hearts,
the mothers of our mothers' hearts.

Even the locusts'.

The Last American New Year
by Samantha Ratcliffe

I thought, *At least we have*
a month before the world ends.
Like a long goodbye might stand right beside
and lead us, bride-like, towards the arrangement.
Just a month of ripe lemons
and out of season honey crisp apples.
A shiny feast of core eyes all aligned.
A whole plump pyramid of unrealistics
Manufactured tart waste.

I'm sick of myself   this year.
Embarrassed like I've slept
all the most important days away.
Sick of our American stomachs,
our languid convictions, our bloodless appeals.
Mourning pacifier vapes instead of babies.
Mourning our spinning mobile distractions,
the metronomic tick tocking in soft heads.
We've gotten good at scrolling past bombs.

We   planted them
while we were busy being bored.
But the new year snuck up on us, didn't it?
As Justice often does. Held us
at gunpoint like only hunger can.

They said the sixth baby froze to death today in Gaza
His father held his premature head like God's
seedless fig and said "cold as ice"
just like we are   now.

An Apology to the Raccoons of Southeast Ohio
by Sullivan Potter

To the raccoons of Jackson, Gallia, Lawrence, Scioto,
Pike, and Vinton counties—
I'm sorry for what I did to your kind.
For what was done through me.
And I'm sorry that the "sensitive, soft"
queer country boy
still living in me
feels the need to write this at all.
Daddy thought coonhounds could tree
on the dead, gnarled oak of our father-son bond—
as if blood trails and skinned pelts
could rouse what had long since rotted at the roots.
He told himself he'd finally want the son he called
"worthless"
once that boy got blood on his hands—
just like he had.
But the blood that dried stickily beneath my fingernails
was yours.
I'm sorry for checking those dog-proof traps
every morning before sixth grade,
for finding you coiled and trembling
in the rising blue hush of dawn.
I'm sorry for gripping Daddy's old Maglite.
Sorry for the cracking of bone and skullcap
you couldn't survive.
He said he didn't want holes in the fur,
but I think he liked seeing me
hurt something
and learn how to hold back the tears.
I'm sorry I couldn't avoid
loading the dogs into Daddy's old Ranger
for a quick turn-out or two,
even when my gut turned over.

If it's any consolation,
I was a pretty sorry dog handler.
I never wanted to shine a beam on a treed hickory—
not because I was afraid to find you there,
but because I knew I would.
And that meant
I'd have to condemn you
to lead and brass.
I'm sorry I grew used to the sickly-sweet stench
of your stiff body,
reeking of sugar and iron.
Sorry for nicking the sinew
that tethered skin to muscle
with my dull blade.
Even hanging muzzle-down,
locked in rigor mortis,
I knew it probably still hurt.
I'm sorry for all the times I tried
to prove my daddy right—
tried to prove I, too, could be
hardened,
cruel,
worth something.
The cruelty he bred into me
wasn't born—
it was inherited.
And it first reddened
in the harm I dealt to you.
I failed at resisting.
My throat choked and swelled,
but I still swung heavy.
My fingers trembled,
but I still pulled the trigger.
My breath caught,
but I still cut deep.
My own cruelty began with your kind.

But I couldn't bear to be what I became—
the one receiving his meanness,
my own silence,
the kind of love that only showed up
after something brutal.
I promise it ends with me.
My children won't raise a gun toward you.
They won't know the sensation
of a knife biting into your wrists.
They won't have to betray their gentleness
for the sake of ruggedness—
or for the approval of a man
who only loves them
because he has to.
So now,
every time I pass your kind
sprawled on the shoulder
of some twisting road,
I'll fall quiet in reverence,
and thank God
it wasn't me
who put you there.

Stories to Tell *by Cara Ellis*

Papaw's boots are by the back porch door,
he wore 'em down in mine number four.
Kept Moonpies in his lunch tin
and a pocketknife his daddy handed him.
He said, "I ain't rich, but I know this land
better than the fella with money in his hand."

Six generations sprung from that well
and we've all got stories to tell
of hardened hands and fightin' songs,
tryin' like hell to right what's wrong.
Coal took more than it ever gave,
sent many men to an early grave.

Called us rednecks 'cause we wore red rags,
tied 'em up tight when the bosses dragged
all the union boys into town one night.
Thought they'd scare us off, but we put up a fight.
The mine's shut down now, you can still hear hums
from the echoes of the workin' man's drum.

Six generations sprung from that well,
and we've all got stories to tell
'bout brother's cough and daddy's limp
and the company doc who ain't worth a cent.
We gave 'em our bodies, they gave us nothin' but debt.
We ain't been licked, not quite yet.

The holler's quiet and the kids have moved on.
I keep a light on 'case they come back home.
We got Sunday songs and borrowed time,
a little bit of luck and a jug of moonshine.

There's a quilt out on the line,
stitched in coal dust and pine,

a square for each kin that was down in the mine.
No riches here, just folks who bleed,
plantin' tomatoes next to their weeds.
Still got pride in this ol' dirt,
even when they took it and left us hurt.

Six generations sprung from that well,
and we've all got stories to tell.
Pass the biscuits, pour ya some sweet tea,
tell y'all all about my family tree.
Dust in our lungs and gospel in our bones,
we ain't fancy, but this is always our home.

Now the preacher says count your blessins',
here's to all of life's lessons.
Amen.

Water Hazard *by Himothy Hazardus*

In the Big City of Louisville, I listen as my classmates talk about how they had to close the floodgates to keep the neighborhoods safe. There are no gates where I come from, only trees that sometimes soak up the rain. We don't have neighborhoods, only hollers and valleys. These days the mountain tops are scarred by strip mining which has diminished their capacity to absorb all that rainwater. I called mama to tell her to put her cell phone in a ziplock bag. This time, FEMA called my uncle who had a wrecker to tell him to "get ready". By the next day, my sister's trailer was all but floating next to the creek. She had managed to make it to Mom's before it was too late. The last I heard from Mama the water got up around her house and the whole family was stuck in the holler, surrounded. A lone truck sat submerged in the bottom of the hillside, land that cradled generations of our lineage. It had been over three days when I finally got that crackly phone call.

"We're okay" she sighed, as if there was more to it.

"Do you have power?" I blurted out.

"No, but we've got the propane heater going…" She sounded hopeful. It was set to start snowing. I gave a silent thanks to the spotty cell towers that seemed to tease the kitchen window with occasional signals. They would be okay.

It was a week before they got the power back on. As kids, we were always waiting for the power to come back to us. Summers on the porch together, just listening to the wind chimes as they danced and laughed in the wind after every big storm.

This time mama was kicking herself for signing up for

that city water. Three weeks went by without a drip
from the faucet. The newsman would come on every
evening just to admit the water was still too
contaminated. Luckily, they had an old washing
machine sitting on the back porch. Uncle Darrell came
over from the house next door and ran a pump from the
creek so they could wash their clothes. Decades pass,
but some things remain the same.

By the time my sister got back to her trailer, the
septic tank was overflowing. The rats from the creek
moved into their swampy house. Floor heaters only
go so far when it comes to drying floors. Even though
they crawled into the underpinning to fix the
plumbing, the rats wouldn't leave. The toes of my
nephews seemed to be their favorite treat.

Most of the citizens of Louisville don't know
anything about that. Unaware that a few hours away,
people still survive like that in 2025. And here I am,
stuck in this city with sewer drains and warming
shelters, and there they are, everyone I've ever loved,
stuck in the valley with all that runoff. They were
lucky enough to have been through this before and
survived. Mamaw always told us all to
listen to what the quiet had to teach us. They know
how to prepare for the worst when the worst
comes knocking. They fill the bathtub with water,
store canned food under their bed frames, and
stockpile propane tanks.

Over time, Appalachians have let their guard down,
trusting faulty promises of solid infrastructure. We know
better than to trust floodgates, the television, our
politicians, even the sky. My family came much too
close to running out of drinkable water this time. As

soon as I could, I drove the four hours just to give them
a handheld emergency water filter that would prevent
water borne illness for the next time the government
failed them. There's always a next time to prepare for.

These city folks watch me carry cat litter jugs filled with
water to my shed and I know they must wonder why. For
them, I am a doomsday prepper. For them, it seems like
an overcautious measure, something they simply don't
think they need. They may be right, for now, these
precautions are extra in a town like Louisville. But
somewhere not too far away, people never stop
preparing. Not too many things separate Kentuckians.
We're all always held in wait under the rich man's
fluctuant remorse, the ever moving helping hand and
willing wallet.

In the back of my mind, I carry the weight, the fragility
of this small life. These stories stick with me and
they're something I can't put down or let go. My people
taught me to prepare, to survive, to save. Regardless of
floodgates or flickering electricity, we know how to
build a fire, how to keep ourselves warm, and how to
gather our own light. I'm from a place where wealth
lives in will, not card or cash but the grit of carving our
own way.

A Hundred Million Boo Radley *by Shaun Turner*

Bless the dreamers, the shouters—
their courage, a bright, blunt knife. Some others are too
tender for the sun. Some bodies are porch-bodies.
On their best days: peeling paint bodies, drawn
shade bodies, sanctuary bodies, absent bodies.
Bodies in the air of a closed room—bodies
that spring alive against the screen —

See how they move in the dark—
a careful architecture of ache and adaptation.

Outside, the glitter kisses the pavement
under the streetlamp. Inside, they keep their
wilderness unmapped—a secret even to the oak tree,
whispered to the moths that batter
the porch light's dusty globe.

Their gifts are precious gifts:
sometimes a poem,
a whittled figure of soap,
a bell jar of blackberries and sweet cornbread
stained with their thumbprint.

A hundred million signs left
on the neighbor's lowest step.
Who needs proof? Scout
their ritual: their window cracked
just enough to smell the rain. You can't watch
the way they touch the small of their own wrist
at dusk—gentle, sure—leading
themselves outside to the moon-drunk porch
all on their own terms.

James *by Willie Edward Taylor Carver Jr.*

The school appointed Mrs. Patricia Doris
my official first year mentor teacher,
who was by any account a tough old bird
hotboxing unfiltered Pall Malls in the parking lot,
the cheap smoke of freedom hovering
about her apple-themed sweater vests
as she came back in before the bell rang.
That lady told me on my very first day
the only thing more important
than not breaking the rules
was never to admit to breaking them,
so I won't say for sure or not
if me and her took turns picking up James
when he walked through the stagnant fog
his freshman year sneakers bobbing through
the 7:00 a.m. road shoulder mud of Route 23
as he made his way to school.

However he made it to the building each day,
he'd end up in my French class after lunch,
where, impervious to verbs or their conjugations,
to nouns and the rules that governed their forms,
to pronouns and articles and relative clauses,
he would quietly sit until his walk home,
watching and waiting from his seat by the window
for Mrs. Doris who foretold the end of our class
with a firmly curved hand cupped around a lighter.

There was no grammar involved in the language fair
that we held at the end of the year.
James looked through a book on French art
that I borrowed for him from the college library,
and he stopped on the impressionists,
said something about them looked really nice,

so I sent him home with a canvas and paint
and a book that held French 19th-century art.

It's not fair
that I can't show now what he brought back
It's not fair
that he had never before held a brush
It's not fair
that I was not prepared to know how to react
It's not fair
that he was able to paint grey matter fog floating across a
fire that looked like blooming, a barn red wall opening to
a fluid expanse of grass and garbage that merged with
the shadows of the hills, the distance of his colors
speaking languages that can't be taught in books,
perspective shown not in space but time that fell back in
on itself in a heavy sigh that melted across the page
It's not fair
that his voice shook the day of the fair
when the judges asked him to explain
why he had chosen to paint
what he had chosen to paint.

Impressionists were these people who wanted to find
something beautiful that was
just normal kinds of places.

   I don't know any beautiful places.

   But I like to burn garbage behind the barn when
I'm feeling stressed out, so I painted that.

   I didn't know I could paint before this.

I hope, James, that Mrs. Doris doesn't mind
that I admit to the world that one of us drove you home

that day
to protect you and the beauty you spread across
        the canvas
from the near constant rain of Route 23,
and I hope that when you remember that year,
you can think of a beautiful place.

Blessed be the Glimmer *by Ariadne Alexis Macquarie*
after Willie Edward Taylor Carver, Jr.

Blessed be the glimmer
of the thin needle beneath
the sickly overhead light.
Blessed be the nectar
beaded at the end of it,
clear & dewy, an angel.
It's that time of week again.
That ritual of stabbing
woman home into the meat
of the thigh. B flinches
but only before the needle
digs beneath the tanned &
ink-mosaiced landscape
of her skin, only before
the pinprick pain becomes
something palpable, akin
to something human. I watch
as L, steady-handed, pushes
slow against the syringe
plunger, guides estrogen
slow into taut muscle.
It's over, Lord, in an instant.
A hush shrouds the room.
We are silent except
for the cicadas hollering
outside, alive & [un]angelic
after hiding for decades, hell
-bent on their fucking frenzy.
That's us, I murmur soft into
our aching silence. *Guys,*
we're alive. We're fucking.
We're cicadas. B & L shoot
me incredulous looks, though

I know they both understand.
We, too, have hunched low
& uncomfortably dormant
in the shells we'd been given,
only to emerge, Christlike,
from our dark tombs after
decades, singing our
praises. We, too, stab
our presence into this
life, making known our
living. We, too, glimmer
in the short span of time
we're given before death
claims us. Life beckons,
& Lord, we claim it.

Branch Rickey: Turkey Creek One-Room Schoolhouse *by Marjorie Maddox*

Seventeen, a farm boy from Duck Run, Branch knew
those schoolhouse walls grew bullies who spat
tobacco juice in teachers' eyes, then beat them bloody
   and bruised.
He took the job anyway, stood up, stood firm

within those schoolhouse walls. Bullies who spat
later sat and learned what the hills and river tell:
take the job anyway, stand up, stand firm,
protect the place you love. The young ones who

sit and listen learn later what the hills and river tell—
what you become you pass on.
Protect the place you love. The young ones who
watch stand up for young ones who watch

who you become in Turkey Creek or Duck Run. Who
knows these fields and mountains knows this.
Watch how the younger ones watch you standing up
to bullies. Home remembers your name,

knows how these fields and hills know you.
These country roads are yours. In every town, every
   ballpark,
name the bullies. Remember your home, your name,
how, at seventeen, just a farm boy from Duck Run,
   you knew

what this country could be, every dirt road, city lot,
   ballpark.
Offer Robinson the game. Each day, stand up, stand
   firm.
At seventeen, farm boy from Duck Run, you knew

how bullies spit, dig in cleats, bruise skin blacker.

Sign Robinson. Watch how he stands up for those who
    watch. Stand firm.
Help save the game you love. Remember your home,
    his name
till bullies spit, cleats spike, skin bruises blacker a little
    less.
Use the job. Stand up. Stand firm. Again. Again. Again.

Young ones, save the world you hate. Remember your
    home. Name
the hills and rivers, what they tell you of yourself
again and again. Take the hard job. Stand up.
    Stand firm.
What you become you pass on.

*Previously published in I Thought I Heard a Cardinal Sing:
Ohio's Appalachian Voices, edited by Kari Gunter-Seymour
(Sheila-Na-Gig Editions, 2022).*

*My great-grand uncle, Branch Rickey, grew up in Duck Run,
Ohio, and, at 17, taught in a one-room schoolhouse in Turkey
Creek, where previous teachers had been bullied and spat
upon by their students. Perhaps this early encounter with
unruly students prepared him to stand up against bullies later
in life. In addition to other roles, he became the General
Manager of the Brooklyn Dodgers and helped break the color
barrier by signing Jackie Robinson to Major League Baseball.*

Rubbed *by Brook West*

I rub people
the wrong way.
My curiosity
like pellets of sand
trapped in your eye.
Wonder, worry, watchful,
a child nicknamed smartass.

A raw wool sweater too tight,
inescapable, soaked in rain.
A tomboy shouldn't have
a pretty face, kiss girls,
waste womanhood.

I fall in love with the moon.
I write her letters
and read the words
to her bright face.
The preacher said,
at Pizza Hut, eye to eye,
crust on his plate,
solemnity in his hands,
a promise in his mouth,
you will burn in Hell, witch.

My manager said
People don't know how to take you.
Taken like a test, unpassable,
taken like innocence, irreversible,
taken like the drawstring
from my sweatpants
at Stoner Creek,
to stay alive, to take you,
if I may, and rub.

The Blood Moon *by Cola Day*

In January, bare mountains on either side of the river split the sky and give God a place to hide among the dying things.

Last time I was back that way, I made good time despite the weather. I was driving northbound on Route 19 and made it to the gorge by evening. When I crossed the bridge, my eyes lifted from the highway to fog filling the valley. At the bottom, whitewater pulsed and wore down the hard places. Maybe next time I would stay.

Suddenly a loud honk threw my car to the left. I swerved past a bulldozer that turned across the bridge to the field where Charity had lived. Years ago, pines veiled it from the highway on one side and the gorge on the other.

In the rearview, I saw other trucks rolling cement over the ground for a cabin, the third to go up in the small clearing. Since the trees were now gone, the cabins sat high above the dirt. Their windows had clear river views for climbers with graduate degrees and out-of-state families wearing Patagonia.

They came more these days, since the federal government bought the land last year and renamed it a park. The river rats caved to investors, and construction sites shot up like weeds. Resorts hired miners Alpha had laid off to kill the copperheads.

Now the visitors came, renting out the mountains for a few days before returning to their suburbs. Besides the men with long beards at hunting season and DNR officers getting calls from funny accents mistaking those same men as bears, nobody really complained. Least of all me.

I made my choices that night of the Blood Moon. It eclipsed on a Sunday morning around the new year–the first year I learned to masturbate and the last I believed in fairies. After school, Charity and I would spend hours hunting for them behind the trailer where she lived. Hidden by the trees, we hoped for beautiful things. We could be stupid enough to look for them.

Beauty dimmed inside the trailer, in front of the Xbox where her cousin screamed every night.

"Why's he always playing to shoot people?" I asked once.

"It helps him get over Iraq," she said.

He moved in after doctors removed part of his brain alongside a tumor. He was on welfare now, gave money to supplement her mother's tips.

In the holiday break before the eclipse, I convinced my mother to let me stay the night with her. The cousin made her reluctant, but I was desperate. I was already doubting in things unseen. If another world was possible, Charity said, the moonlight could reveal it.

My mother bargained, "As long as you still go to church."

That night at Charity's, we waited until her cousin passed out on the couch. Together we opened her window. Into the darkness, we stepped without shoes between dried marigolds in Styrofoam cups on her windowsill.

She wished us luck with a single kiss on my left cheek.

We walked on, frozen grass pulling all feeling from our toes. I watched for the glitter of broken glass or needles, thinking of the boy living out of his black F-150 down the road. Usually we crouched to search but Charity stood tall, looking upward.

Her pupils widened to the night, curtained by silky bangs that spilled onto a red, freckled nose. I thought of strawberries and her bare legs in June. Following her eyes, I saw it.

The Blood Moon was a brown ball held fast by bright stars pinned to the sky. Like dogs we cocked our heads, waiting quietly as the moonlight washed over us. In the dark her breath slipped from her nose in little silver clouds. I watched her and placed my cold hand to my cheek where she had kissed me earlier.

Why had she done that?

I wanted to go back inside.

"When should we leave?" I asked.

"Where else would we go?" she replied.

Before I could answer, a faint echo of trickling water startled us. We looked back to the trailer and saw her cousin's shadow pissing off the porch.

The moment he looked back at us, Charity squealed. Sprinting, she disappeared into the night without looking back. I started after her. Unable to feel my feet, I caught a sharp rock and fell over. Suddenly something warm and sticky oozed between my toes.

Her cousin stood over me. He smelled like rotten bread.

"Why y'all out in this goddamn field," he muttered. I watched his face and thought of a bloated fish I found washed up on the riverbank last summer.

"Just looking," I whispered, scanning the field for Charity.

He seemed to talk to himself, though he was talking to me.

"Look at you, lookin like that at your big age in my house, girl."

He then crouched low. His sweaty fingers gripped my cut foot hard. One by one they crawled up to my knee like spiders. Then my thigh.

He froze. A bright beam of light from the road lit up the field. It shone on the soft part of his skull that the tumor had eaten away. The black F-150 slowed, and the boy driving stared with squinted eyes. Without speaking, Charity's cousin retreated in the grass like a frightened animal. I stood still and watched him crawl back through the field to the trailer.

Beyond the bony trees, I heard the highway echo. It was a quiet hum only possible in the dead of winter, in the silence that settles after the cicadas and before the peepers. Hikers, truck drivers, and travelers passing through the gorge. A wild pause, the gap where the ugliness sets in and clouds the way.

On the other side, I thought, lay the unseen things. Hope had to be there, if not in the inbetween.

When I finally returned to Charity's room, she was undressing on the bed. It smelled like cinnamon from wax tarts my mother gifted her mother on the anniversary of their sobriety.

"Where the hell were you?" she laughed. I grabbed a stray napkin and wrapped my cut, explaining the fall but forgetting the rest. She drifted asleep, but I lay awake measuring the distance in a rift. How much, after all, can hide in the break between ourselves and what we throw away?

My mother came in the early morning to take me to church. As we drove southbound over the bridge, a hot crimson sun rose just beyond the barren valley. It shimmered on the pines, burning away the purple mist that rose from the river. I followed its fuzzy glow, dared it to blind me.

With every mile we drove further away, the mountains became more beautiful. Like a stranger I keep going, so they are beautiful to me, still.

The Prettiest Please *by Brandon Sun Eagle Jent*

For the country women who raised me

I was going to give birth to my prettiest please, swaddle
     it
like the crankiest baby. Hospital corners, a delicate
     knowing.
I would've babied it the way his mother did her only
     son,

the way he expected his ex-wife to manage
the work shirt creases, his piss-poor aim
along the toilet seat. He hadn't been with a man before

me, expecting I would walk the same pearl-chested
mile in a pair of pumps never sold in my size.
Dolly, not Dollar Store. He loved my spiral curls,

the docile melodies from my high-strung larynx.
He hated my backwards backtalk, the survival
skill of country women he found unrefined as knotty

pine that never knew polish. My tongue is my aunt's
autopsies, her knife sliding down deer bellies. Two-
     Spirit
and trans, she tanned buck hides in their own brains and
     piss,

sun-bleached them white on our trailer park porch. My
     words carve
conversations like the tread of my mother's canvas Keds

the night she marched down those same porch steps,

sped her Chevy past the FLORENCE Y'ALL water
        tower
and left that motherfucker for good this time—
his three spawn squalling in her backseat, his handprints

garnet on her limp left arm. My silence is the hymnal
of my never-quiet mamaw cough-closing suitcases
and teaching the trunk to whisper the day she escaped
        papaw

without a scratch. I had planned out the birth of my
        prettiest please,
from belly-knot conception to quiver-lipped delivery.
But I remembered Loretta and "The Pill" and aborted the
        bastard.

He said he wanted Dolly, wound up with Dollar Store.
That twink he's texting could never be Jolene.

For Lil *by Shiloh Stump*

Blessed are the holler rats
turned gutter punks
turned sanctified carriers
of narcan and cast iron—

Every rat making paradise
from what kings leave behind
is my kin

Every skag shooter
Every street angel of death
and OD Revivialist
Every no-good-low-down
Black-Brown-red-white
trash who's ever opened
their own veins is my
sibling

So, come
all ye' holler rats
ye' rez rats
hood rats and trailer trash
come all my redneck sissies
and cross dressing bubbies
my hostile heatherns
turned heavenly hellraisers
come

We shape our lives
with the chalk outlines
of those who are leaving,
leaving,
gone

We shape our grief
with the shaking hands
of those who remember
for when one of us rats is lost,
who better than us
to remain?

Alchemy *by NitaJade*

I've finally figured out how to alchemize the wind:
      it starts with water
      (*it always starts with water.*)
      take the miracle that carries your blood
      the anxious pool at the base of your belly
      & send it up the back of your throat.
      there, taste it. grimace at the bile
      but keep going. the truth that sits beneath
      the bitter is what you're aiming to extract.
      once you've swished that around
      the right words will settle mid-tongue.
      that's when you breathe, darlin'
      breathe the truth into the air.
      open a window so it catches on a breeze
      & that breeze will find the feathers of a crow
      who is bored with all the shit going on earthside
      so she plays on the wind.
      when released, her wings
      — her wings! —
      will catch a gale & surf
      from the blue grass
                           to the blue ridge
      & back again.
This is how you carry broken circles to your mother.
This is how silence, broken, carries you both.

Teach Me To Dance Because Bodies Never Lie
by Marianne Peel

He was always the life of the party, my Uncle Harry.
After a few highballs—Cutty Sark and soda—he would
kick off his loafers, loosen his dentures, just a little, and
in his stocking feet, launch into the Buck Time Step on
the carpet. He'd make clicking sounds by rattling his
loose dentures. Teeth tapping against teeth.

My mama put me to bed the night before,
pink sponge rollers plastered to my head,
and I was a walking-talking Shirley Temple holding
Uncle Harry's hand, tapping out the Alexander on that
rug. My father called Uncle Harry a bullshitter behind
his back. *Dancing is like dreaming with your feet,*
my Uncle Harry used to say. There was always the
promise of Coney Island Amusement Park: cotton candy
on a stick, elephant ears dredged in powdered sugar.
The promise of a Ferris wheel ride after dark.
All those lights winking on the spokes. Sitting in that
bucket seat together, licking cotton candy sugar off our
fingers. Calliope music as I pumped my legs.
I longed to swing among the stars, touch my toes
to the edge of the summer moon.

But when we visited him in hospital, he was drenched
with night sweats. White patches on his gums, his
tongue, even the lining of his mouth. Purple splotches on
his eyelids. His bourbon belly now gone. A shriveled up
version of himself in a fetal position. Trying to crawl
back into his mama's womb. But his mama was a
wooden spoon kind of woman, hair coiled in an
unyielding bun at the base of her neck.
She'd kicked him to the curb long ago.

Uncle Harry's partner paced the hall outside the hospital
room. Monogrammed handkerchief in his jacket pocket.
His hands so beautifully manicured. Always such clean
and rounded nails. But in his pacing, he'd shredded his
cuticles. Blood on his knuckles. Hands stuffed into his
pockets. So much pacing.

Fluid gathered at the back of Uncle Harry's throat.
Raspy voice now, like dry leaves crumpled in his mouth.
I served him ice chips from a Styrofoam cup.
Offered water on a sponge. Rubbed his feet with aloe
and lanolin. Smoothed petroleum jelly
between bruised toes.

Cause of death on Uncle Harry's certificate: pneumonia.
I knew there was more. Because no one touched
the purple sores, his emaciated torso.
Because no one mentioned
the week of diarrhea,
the blisters on his cracked lips.
Because no one admitted
how tired he was.
So damn tired.

At the memorial service, all they said about his partner
was that *he made a damn good spaghetti.*
Meatballs a comingling of beef and pork.
Homemade fettuccine. And the basil. So much basil.

And he could dance. Mostly the soft shoe.
With a glass of cabernet sauvignon in one hand,
his other hand around Uncle Harry's waist.
Pasta bowls piled high in the sink.
So close. Dancing.
Whistling a made-up tune.
He pulled my Uncle Harry in.

A Letter, With Love, to The Self-Anointed
by Thailan Franklin

My love is feminine. My love is masculine. My love has
no rough edges or jagged ends. My love does not hold
shape, but is every shape. My love is divinity. My love is
prayer and conjure, heaven and hell—purgatory, even.
My love is everything that you pray to your god
for—everything that you pray to your god about.
My love is the embodied manifestation of your wildest dreams
and your greatest fears.

You will never understand Love: how it holds your insecurities
and your confidences, how it blankets every blemish, and how
it still encourages every potential refinement. Your love learned
to walk on water through mine. Your love learned to part seas,
heal the sick, and give sight to the blind. My love, you say,
invented waves: diseases to be cured and veils to be lifted. My
love holds every truth that your love is too weak to bear. My
love is not fragile. My love is thick roots running through tight
soil—grounded. My love is sustained.

Be there no book, be there no building, be there no history. My
love is the bible, my love is the palace, my love is the evidence.
The proof.

Your love is a false prophet, parading its stolen powers
through hive minds.

My love is the glow—
surrounding every living thing,
only noticed through deep breaths
and planted soles.

Instructions For Ranking Your Sins
by Jay McCoy

document your sins

*Now the works of the flesh
are manifest, which are these:*

write them down / ink
to parchment or blood
to lambskin / choose
your instruments wisely

*adultery, fornication, uncleanness,
lasciviousness, idolatry, witchcraft,
hatred, variance, emulations, wrath,*

this is a physical exercise
to manifest on the page
be intentional / be absolute
be precise / explain each
envy / savor each variance

*strife, seditions, heresies, envyings,
murders, drunkenness, revellings,
and such like:*

surround / capture
the wretched / ensconce
the beautiful / be specific

*Being filled with all unrighteousness,
fornication, wickedness, covetousness,
maliciousness; full of envy, murder,*

mine each maliciousness
deeply / completely exploit
every emotion

debate, deceit, malignity; whisperers,
backbiters, haters of God, spiteful,
proud, boasters, inventors of evil things,

allow time to simmer / to
fester / to bloom / Consider
the pleasure drawn when
teeth meets flesh at 3 am

without understanding, disobedient to parents,
covenant breakers, without natural affection,
implacable, unmerciful:

rank these same sins
rate each offense / zero
to infinity

Knowing this, that the law is not made
for a righteous man, but for the lawless
and disobedient, for the ungodly and for
sinners, for unholy and profane,

categorize these sins
if you must / from most
subversive to least
unpleasant

for murderers of fathers and murderers of mothers,
for manslayers, for whoremongers, for them that defile
themselves with mankind, for menstealers, for liars,

weigh them / heavy
to light / elephantine
to ethereal

for perjured persons, and if there be any
other thing that is contrary to sound doctrine;
But the fearful and unbelieving,

contemplate their value

and the abominable, and murderers,

and yours

and whoremongers, and sorcerers,

consider their worth

and idolaters, and all liars,

and yours

shall have their part in the lake

pray

which burneth with fire and brimstone:

pray

which is the second death.

pray

64

Plea *by Beth Feagan*

Let me roll on through to the wide silver sea
Let me rise on up through the light green leaves
Let me hurtle on in through the quiet,
dripping trees
       spiderwebs coating my face
       rooted down into this place
Let me run toward the clearing where
I am giving birth
Let me sing with the whippoorwill's
song in my mouth
Let me sit cross-legged on the warm,
mossy earth
       and remember I'm clay
       and pray to stay free

The Grammar of Gayness in Eastern Kentucky
by Eric Morris

A grammar is a system of rules that define the
possibilities of existence for a language, a group of
people, or a society that employs either of those two
things. Grammars are unifying instead of excluding,
descriptive instead of prescriptive, and, more often than
not, used incorrectly even by people with a great
familiarity with something they interact with each day.
Even if all of those contradictions are true, a grammar
seemed the best system to use to elaborate upon what it
means to be gay in the rurality that Eastern Kentucky
encompasses, mainly due to the nature of how this place
allows those of us in this community to define our own
rules for existence instead of applying definitions created
from outside communities.

The geography of this region might terrify an outsider
who might label pockets of our state as "isolated" or "cut
off," yet the long hollers that join us together instead act
as tributaries to larger streams and rivers of thought.
Like water itself, individuals cohere and move together
toward goals that benefit more than a single person,
although we learn a certain type of self-sufficiency here
that urges us to survive on our own as much as possible.
Rurality has always valued individuals being able to
support themselves, but many rural residents realize that
we can choose to follow that path instead of allowing
other circumstances to force us down this track as our
only recourse. Strength exists in that option to choose.
We might call this idea interdependent isolationism—we
choose our own individual, independent lives, but we
come together in times of need—like disasters,
marriages, divorces, or whatever—or in times of
want—like holidays, social gatherings, and other
positive events. We create nonprofits, clubs, and

celebrations of our own, on our own terms; does it not make sense that we could create our own communities, too?

Where we tend to encounter difficulties is when those communities or categories brush against the outside world. This tendency is nothing new for rural areas, but that effect is magnified whenever we incorporate a community that many people throughout the world have labeled as something outside the realm of the normal. For many people who consider their lives illustrations of banality or regularity, gayness or transness would be an aspect of identity that they would push into one of those "other" categories. Rural gay citizens might try to find examples from the rest of the world to define themselves, and they may discover that urbanites possess a very different idea of what being gay might look like than their rural compatriots. The truth is, of course, that there are many different types of gays, just as there are many types of people. So many members of our community seek membership in societies that they only visit two or three times a year, but know they will not gain access, so they settle somewhere in the middle, like in the more urban cities an hour or two from where they grew up. This compromise does bring them the best of both worlds in many ways, but another option exists that so many overlook when they consider this pathway a failure. What is this other option? It is the chance to create their own grammar, their own rules. And we each have that ability here in Eastern Kentucky. So, you do not fit in one of the preconceived categories defined by popular media or communities from abroad that you engage with? Create your own. You only need one other example to give your ideas legitimacy, and merit here can be earned whenever categories gain relevance as people see examples in their everyday lives. Give your

grammar legitimacy by surviving even when others may
try to convince you to do otherwise.

We devise our own rules and our own grammar to
connect with those people who possess the qualities we
also deem important. Our geography has enabled us to
do this by forcing us to forge connections across
boundaries, barriers, and time, for we need those
connections to hold true when we encounter someone we
may only meet a few times a year, especially if we want
to grow closer to others in our community. This system
for seeing others relates back to one of the most
important aspects of grammar that we can pass down to
others and remind them: Grammar describes our
experiences in the world as they are, not as they "should
be" according to someone's perceptions. If this
definition does not sit well with you, then maybe you
can find the power that most Eastern Kentucky gays
know and form your own rules and your own grammar
to live by.

a perfect day *by christiana cantrell*

if i could have one day to be fully myself,
i reckon my chest would be flat.
i would go fishing and catch lots with my dad,
and we wouldn't even talk about That.
i would sing with my momma, steal kisses from
my lady, and make my siblings' children laugh.
not once through the day would they gawk at me
awkwardly walking with the legs of a baby giraffe.

no, i'd be confident, and witty, and weaving
my words together seamlessly. i'd go when i wanted
and stay when i didn't. i'd let myself make a few bad
decisions. i'd highlight the kindness, the love that
surrounds us, the way Earth's sweet soil gives us
sustenance, the trees, the air we breathe. i'd bust up the
shipping routes, the lobby mouths, the war machine and
its corporate greed. they'd tremble in fear
of the power We yield.

i'd duet with my pal Hippi, but now he'd have
a house. i'd get to introduce my lover as my wife
instead of my spouse. let myself out of the meeting
rooms, and further into serving more food.
for i know the law will crumble and the People will still
hunger. i'd like to

fill their bellies & souls,
come home and reflect in the evening,
smoke and journal, bleed on paper,
plan a hiking trip, plan a potluck,
make a playlist, find somewhere new to tinker,
find the words to express that only we
can save us.

get more tattoos, a motorcycle,
and, finally, that library degree.
connect the dots,
blur the lines,
get more people free.

if i was fully me for a day,
it'd be hard to let it all go—
the past and the way it haunts me,
or the desire for who i truly am.
not sure if i'll ever see that day,
but, boy,
ain't it a hell of a plan?

What is the South to an Outsider
by Emily M. Goldsmith

Wind in the escaped hairs of my french braid,
the pitter-patter of our feet hitting sun-burned concrete,
springing from one imagined adventure
to the next.

My young years were grass staining, tree climbing,
railroad minding, bush hiding, blackberry picking,
swamp sitting, running home at sunset before
the streetlights lit up our neighborhood
and Mama served dinner.

My palms dirty and shirt ripped, scrapes up and down
my legs, I knew the summers like the books I read
again and again on bad weather days.

Church on Sunday mornings, sure, matching outfits that
tugged and pulled. Temper tantrums on the way and *I
brought you into this world, I can take you out.*

Barbeques, crawfish boils, corn on the cob,
mashed potatoes, and double servings of pastalaya.

There may have been a *bless your heart* or *how far he
strayed,* but there was also a full crew to clean
your house up after a hurricane, free of charge,
and always somebody to watch your kids.

After a funeral? You'd be fed for days. Your neighbors
checking in and seeing if they need to mow the lawn and
you didn't even have to know them well.

A nod hello from far away, a *how you doing,*
a stop to chat in the grocery store.

As a kid, I would pull my mom's hand if she talked too
long. I'd ask, *who was that*? She'd say, *Oh,*
your dad's second cousin.

For me, everything lives and thrives in in-between
spaces. What is the South to an outsider?
Bugs they don't know the names for and multiplicity
they can't understand. What is the South to me?

Lightning bugs lighting up dusk skies,
long steady night sounds of leopard
frogs or crickets, bull frogs after a good
rain, humid air, colorful skies, family
gatherings, cemetery grounds, reckoning
and reconciliation, where I first fell in
love, where I'll be buried when it all ends.

Rally Round the Golden Bull *by Ell Havoc*

Tell me, which side are you on?
Your silence is acceptance
the plague, the gallows,
the rich man's feast,
Devils wearing robes of priests.

Wolves in the temple, feeding greed
on every lamb they swore to lead.

Come kneel with those
they cast aside—
the broken, the bruised,
the crucified.
Fake shepherds,
blood-stained ties,
preaching peace with empty eyes.

Watch them turn the other cheek
while children die at their feet.

Who sold the truth?
They did.

Who bought the cross?
They bid.

Who burned the Saints?
You know the drill—

They rally 'round the golden bull
and kill kill kill.

Deadman's Curve *by C.A. Osborne*

I was my Father when I got my teeth yanked out,
spilling them all over Deadman's Curve. Picking them
up, shoving them back in, hoping I was asleep because I
took too many pain pills.

Sharp, one-lane roads widened and smoothed out for
yuppies moving here. But I'm unhinged in my room,
taking Benadryl until I feel seen, sleeping like I'm dead
until I'm puking out a dream.

Sharp, one-way moods, flattened and smoothed out for
parents trying to move on. They're unhinged in their
room. Taking pills to not be seen, until they're puking
out the inseams of my childhood.

So fucking bored. Banging my head on the walls.
Watching the depression sneak in with wolf spider legs,
crawling all over me. Yelling, screaming, brain activity
dimmed.

Suddenly!

The golden, burning mania drags me to the sun, melting
my skin until I'm dripping in the kitchen and begging for
help. Bone naked in front of the only goddamn people I
ever see, disgustingly psychotic in front of my family.

Put me in the Danger Ranger, take me to the river.
Baptize me in the murky mud, christen me in
Kentucky Gentleman, run that trot line.
Hook my deteriorating mind as the bait,
run that trot line. Sliced my thumb, run that trot
line. Bled on every chicken liver tossed away,
run that trot line.

Richest county in the state. Poorest family I know.
Watching depressed farmland frantically subdividing
into subdivisions.

Seventeen, I couldn't tell. Oldham County and I were
headed for hell. Depression deer ticks sucking on all I
had to give, manic heatwave sapping my soul.

Now even still, when my mind is on fire,
everything is ash, I sprint to the county line and hide
with my parents behind the few trees left alive.

Good American Speech *by Alicia Wright*

It's cicadas or it's crickets
or it's something else entirely—
it's whatever a peeper is.

I lost it somewhere, mashed it to paste
between my teeth—no buggy, no crawdad,
nobody redding up the table for supper,

but something Mid-Atlantic—
crooked on the tongue and never fit
enough for the stage.

We're all Shakespeare in the foothills
here, damp clover clinging to our ankles,
but the crick bleeds in:

I can't explain the night without it,
or the jellied mass of eggs sprouting limbs
and crawling for the hemlock,

can't tell the truth about the water's bite
or our clothes in wrinkled piles on the bank.

I can't spell the name of the bone-white shells
raked by the palmful from the silt,
thin as fingernails, quiet as parentheses.

Why I Write Poetry *by Marianne Worthington*
after Major Jackson

Because when I eat Cheerios for breakfast, the dog
    stands
beside me, balancing on three legs without moving,

trusting me to give her the milky remains. Because I
    miss
seeing the October leaves in the woods surrounding

my cousin's house by the lake. Because I miss
seeing my cousin who died violently and suddenly.

Because I will never get over her death. Because
my blood family is very small, and getting smaller.

I write poetry to chase after the words describing
East Tennessee in summer. No greener place

exists on earth. Because Dolly Parton, James Agee,
Cormac McCarthy, Brownie McGhee, and Beauford
    Delaney

are from the same place as I am. Because the
    mockingbirds
are furious all the time. I write poetry because the
    current

image system where I live is [still!] Trump flags, pain
clinics, jeep rallies, Patriot churches, and Dollar
    Generals.

Because it is the end of February, and I am still waiting
for the groundhog who lives next door to wake and come

out of her tunnels. Because her babies will sunbathe
in the mornings on my neighbor's deck. Because baby

groundhogs sploot like corgis. I write poetry because
if I didn't, I would just caffeinate all day. Because

when the bluebirds gather on the roof outside my
    window,
 they take turns diving delicately into the puddle to
    bathe.

Transmission *by Flossie Hedges*

I have 64 great, great,
great, great grandparents.

In their crowded parlor, a party of glassine and scrim,
there is a woman who held in her a woman who fed
at her chest a man who perpetually re-adjusted the home
of the germ of a child whose child grew to watch
Haystacks Calhoun on a screen as thick as a Ball jar.

She said she could only love a man
with a round body and coal black hair.

Sitting on a pop case and stretching the bird bones
of her feet until they cracked like kindling does,
she described her Saturdays searching for him
at dance halls and service stations,
following the fractured trails
of classmates' cousins and salesmen in from the city.

She asked around purposively,
with my origin at risk.

And now, before I cross Kentucky to watch
pockmarked men in neoprene throw their bodies
at each other like badly weighted wiper blades,
I pluck the glass-white threads from my temples
and push my broad hand across the growing night.

Hush *by Amanda Jo Slone*

Her story has been told for generations. No one remembers the first time they heard it. I grew up in this holler, where she is as real as I am. I tell her story. We all do. Over time, it has become our own—a part of a collective history we claim and share. She is ours, and we insert ourselves into her narrative.

We start close to midnight. There is a late autumn storm, the kind that still holds a bit of warmth in winds that swirl leaves in the air. Rain thrums on the ceiling. Fog clings to the windows, and the air is thick in the tiny cabin. We sit in the front room, at the foot of the rocker where she is holding the baby. The baby cries in jagged snubbing breaths. Mother rocks a little faster, her frail hand pats a rhythm on a clean cloth bottom. The cry rises in a shrill alarm. We clench our jaws. We begin to sweat. We sit next to her, the mother, and feel her frustration. She has changed, fed, and rocked, and still the screaming grows. There is something in the baby's throat—anguish or anger—the kind of cry that is hurled in accusation. We might sweep our eyes around the cluttered cabin, but we know she is alone. We know the way she hides the child from prying eyes, wrapped up in an apron, when she leaves home. The whole holler knows the gossip, and what they do not know, they invent.

We lean in close to the mother, her worn-out whispered pleas hot and tickling on our ears. We sit with her and feel the weight of every judgment, the crush of every love gone wrong. We see the tears at the corners of her eyes. She cannot wipe them away, so they roll down her cheeks, pool up in wrinkled folds of baby neck. Mother and child cry together. It is getting closer to midnight, and we stretch our mouths in her yawn. We might even begin to slip, but we jerk awake when we feel her mother arms fold and rock as she wraps the apron tight, a suffocating swaddle.

We take the long walk with her down Laurel Fork. We do not walk beside her, but we follow close behind. Close enough to still hear the muffled cries. We stop between two trees that stretch naked limbs toward the moon. Maybe we dig with her. We take up a tiny garden trowel and scratch at the mud. Our fingernails fill up, and we leave a trail of dirt on our skin as we wipe away the rain and the sweat and probably the tears that gather on our face. We do not help her tuck the baby in. She must do that part alone. We see her place the bundle beneath the ground. She is tender, and we turn away out of embarrassment or deniability. She uses her hands to scoop the blanket dirt. She gives the mound a pat. It is quiet. We know she will take her own life next, but we do not extend a hand to her. We leave. We will tell the story. We will wave our muddy hands and speculate her motive, but we will not witness the end.

Everyone knows that at midnight, on nights like these, the baby still cries. Throughout our lives, we will make the pilgrimage to Laurel Fork on rainy nights to try to hear for ourselves. Once with our uncle, who swears he heard the cries, and we believe him, though he has a complicated relationship with substances and the truth. Once with a group of high school friends who are spooked by the dark and laugh at the story, but leave before the clock strikes twelve. Once with a boy who thinks we might be scared and pulls us close to slip a hand under our blouse, but vows he is listening as we talk about her. And only this once alone.

My own children are asleep at home. There is no one else to wonder where I'm going, though people will talk. I drive over Beauny Mountain, by James France's Holler, and Jim Swiney's Branch. I live in a place where everything is named. I know what to call every bump and twist in the narrow half-lane road. I recite them as I drive. The only name I do not know is hers. Her name is lost to time, to ghost mother memory.

The moon is reaching its highest point when I park the car beneath the trees. I sit in the dark with the windows down and the doors locked. I listen. I think of pain, of buried grief, of unnamed suffering. I wonder if she was real, if she loved her baby. I wonder if she was ever loved, if I have been. I wonder how much the story has changed over time, how much of it is our fault. I wonder about the difference between honor, memory, and shame. I wonder what other people think, what I will tell my children when they ask about her. The night is still and black. The crying comes at midnight. It is a low guttural cry that swells from body and spirit. My shoulders are tight, and I feel the sting of tears, the barb of shame, and the prick of regret, but I do not know whose they are.

Hell in a Handbasket *by Bayley Hope Amburgey*

"Now I lay me down to sleep,
I pray the Lord my soul to keep.
If I should die before I wake,
I pray the Lord my soul to take,"

are words I memorized when I was a toddler.

Growing up in a Pentecostal household in
Eastern Kentucky, this wasn't unusual. Now, at 27 and
living with a deep-rooted fear of death and a diagnosis of
existential OCD, it seems outright insane.

Why should a young child be taught chants about where
their soul will go after death?

As a child, you barely understand death, but as a
Pentecostal child, you are taught to fear it early. Saying
those culty, ritualistic type chants about your soul's
landing place each night was required. For what if you, a
small child, were to die in your sleep without saying
your prayer? Would that mean you're going to hell?

What if you ate without saying grace—would you choke
on your Texas Roadhouse roll and go straight to hell?

Because the threat of "going to hell" can apply to any
sin, it made ordinary, earthly pleasures impossible. Eat
too much? Going to hell. Gossip? Going to hell.
Pre-marital sex— or even thoughts of sex? Straight to
hell! And for God's sake, don't touch yourself. Or be
gay. That's a first-class ticket to hell!

I learned to suppress myself. My thoughts, my questions,
my concerns, the feelings at the pit of my heart and

stomach… I suppressed my voice, my sexuality, any of my desires to have fun like the other kids.

Because I was scared of hell, and being myself meant going there.

When they staged "test runs" of the rapture at church camp and said nightly death prayers, how can the first thing on your mind not be your inevitable death? And more importantly… what if I go to hell?

But one day you wake up and realize the very people who instilled that fear do plenty of things that—by their own rules—could send them to hell: lying, judgment, adultery, greed… the list goes on.

If those are the people who get to go to heaven, and if going to heaven means I can never be myself—never be truly free here on earth—then…

send me to hell in a handbasket.

an abundance of blue jays *by Jessica Powers*

trees reaching into gray open sky—my family
gathering on the porch to watch the jays eat their peanuts
it's their thanksgiving too little brother says
bright blue flitting through bare branches
and god, I miss the porch even as I am standing right
here. how I ache for the thing as I am inside of it:
the creak of old wood, a night walk to the golf course for
no better reason than the full moon, my bare feet in the
grass, autumn-haired boys from high school shouting
on the river right before they are gone forever,
cicadas in the heat, and near-soundless
snow in the winter. how I can still remember the way to
your house—there's a forever map of country roads I
can't let go of. little brother hefts another handful of
peanuts toward the birds and I know
I am hungry as a blue jay for home.

Someone's Baby *by Charlotte Isenberg*

The silent writhing,
death-defying, self-sacrificing
miracle of motherhood.

What a cruel joke, what a punchline,
to let me hold it, perfect,
knowing it growing would kill us both.

I have nothing for you now. I am wire and bile
and wrung-out edges.
My only hope, my sweet summer star, is to take you far,
far away from this.

The pills are bitter and my spit is viscera, so I sink low
to the floor for its cold against my skin.

I am a warm, aching pool, profoundly alone for the
privilege of bleeding out beside the toilet because they
decided a doctor's office is too dangerous.

I smile, knowing I am also an animal body clawing to a
single-track survival that no law could stop.

I am free in spirit, in spite, like the dust after the flood,
like the kudzu, like my trailing blood.

Oh Arthur, oh Sylvia, please come back when I get
clean, when I am new.
Thank you. I'm sorry.
I am someone's baby too.

Breathing Space *by Melissa Helton*

I am driving and daydreaming in the early lilac
sunrise of how the girl's finger traced the shape

of my earlobe, how she revelled because I couldn't
help but tilt forward and wait for her answer,

      and I see the eastern cottontail sitting
      on the highway's white edge line, a little
      puff along the rumble strip, and I lift my foot,
      just briefly, off the gas.

      At this moment, the rabbit has 360 degrees
      of options, like the girl did then,
      radii spoking out from a center like solar rays

      spoking from the core's convection.
      They can run in any direction, the rabbit
      on the highway, the girl answering
      my *do you want me.*

         She could say *yes*, say *not like this*, say *it
         depends*, say *not anymore*, say *let's see
         what happens tomorrow.*

All sense would dictate the rabbit and the girl
would run a direction that would not result

in a crunch beneath my car tire when they finally
spark into that instinct zig zag.

      The moment ticks forward
      and they both move.

         I hold my foot off the gas
         to see what will happen.

Pineville *by Caitlin Valentine*

Gaggles of cousins and kin
Congregate giddily on mossy stools.
An angelic glow descends through the lace
Of a viridian canopy high above golden crowns.

Granny calls me her *Precious Moments* Baby,
I'm her "Buttercup Princess."
I bloom over to her Princesses Daisy and Rose,
We are a generational court, an Appalachian bouquet.

Taking many breaks from crawdaddin'
To share the most recent family drama.
Folks are always breaking up, acting up, toking up,
Worse.

An aunt screeches at a water moccasin,
Dozens of hillfolk roar with laughter.
A seemingly identical family
Waves to ours from across the way,
They'll call the cops on us later.

Two types of smoke waltz together,
Marlboros and a heavily seasoned fish-fry.
Cayenne and paprika invite a stomach rumble
As I glide off a boulder with invisible fairy wings.

Reunion uniforms, proudly worn.
A vintage Wildcats, or a number three, t-shirt will do.
When barefooted in a creek,
Any inklings of avarice evaporate with the dew.

A blank space where the plastic cutlery was designated,
Someone slipped n' fell into vacation-mode too early.
None of us feel too prissy to eat with our hands.

Ambrosia should be eaten by the handful anyway.

Here, in the tranquil babbles
Floating amongst a luscious thicket,
Cradled by mountains older than the thicket itself,
No weapon formed against us shall prosper.

Neglected and targeted by men in suits,
Every trauma systemically designed and distributed.
We are susceptible to trust and hope.
Our hearts may palpitate, but forever beat as one.

When Lola Comes to Town *by Ellie Bee*

You wouldn't know by the way my Lola
tends her native flower garden,
reuses all the containers,
even the ones *they* say you can't.
Adorned head to toe with stickers,
knows the roadways like lines on my niece's hand—
though she ain't from here.

You may know by the way she
dances in her rollator,
tells family to *mind their business!*
with furrowed brows and scrunched lips,
because we are all just trying to survive;
needs to know where your love is stored—
she grew up 'round gay folk.

You must know by the way she
loves the family of the family of your love,
cleans every crevice of every bone,
needing only the tools this ground gave,
in ten shovels and shark teeth;
gives family recipes to the stranger—
she never left the island.

I know
when she stops in Corbin for gas
on her way to visit us
they ask, "Now where *you* from?"
She replies, "The same place as you."

Christmas in Iowa *by Nefi Sanchez*

If wisemen sought Him today
They would be brown boys on bikes
Humming through Midwestern roads
Broken English lookalikes
They'd follow a shattered star
Whose sparks scatter in streetlights
Honey drops of joy for bugs
Sidewalk laughter on still nights
And their gold, frankincense, and myrrh
Would be made into one embrace
Of thin chains and cheap cologne
Holding baby Jesus' face
If angels sang out today
They'd be gas station cashiers,
Someone's mom who knows my name
Even after all these years
They'd descend, glowing different
With BP's neon lights
Honey drops of joy for bugs
Parked car laughter on still nights
And all their songs of praises
They'd cough out of tune and dry
Soft familiarity
Soothing baby Jesus' cry
If shepherds kept watch today
They'd be can-collecting men
Penny-scraping local bins
Over and over again

Their fears'd find heavenly peace
In paying cars' safe warm lights
Honey drops of joy for bugs
Streetside laughter on still nights
And the little lambs they watch

Would be a check of loose crumbs
Crumbled in their dust-caked coat
Until baby Jesus comes
If Jesus was born today
It'd be in a lowly place
With plain and simple people
Making great and precious space
Like trailer parks' gravel roads
Holding him in lone porchlights
Honey drops of joy for bugs
Porchlight laughter on still nights
His manager and all its guests,
He'd still want them equally
He'd watch them shift year to year
And still always baby Jesus be

Room 3 *by Mark Boykin*

Triply hard pencils are for artists
and those of us with dense hands.
In room 3, I encourage certified
hard water to get softer in my

Mr. Coffee-brand coffeemaker,
on my one day off a jackhammer
sketching cracks in this city cobbled
together on a silt bed; every year

the foundation scuttles southward.
I've long felt they should repair
the fiberglass insulation but I didn't
make a fuss because… some things

need to stay the same, for god's sakes,
they'll boot agitated popcorn paint chips,
fracking poison mineral cloisters, sowing
robot cotton candy in my fucking carpet,

worse manners than my pops, worse-spoken,
jeez. He says, "You got to be your own carpenter,
'cause whether cold or hot, you'll drink the coffee,"
before plastic letters first bubbled from below:

UNDER CONSTRUCTION; NO TRESPASSING
Carefully glowing uniform off, on rack.
Run humming cards over indiscreet readers,
full pockets from knockabout catering,

climb escape ladders home, try at stilling this city.
A second per scribble. Street-level renditions swallow
throats' lumps, caught, held
gently with graphite; every year, the foundation…

Digressions *by Jude DeWalt*

Staggering out into the driveway,
it's mostly gravel and chicken shit,
so dark that I can't see the ground.
I unlock my car,
making it my lighthouse,

backing out for sixty feet,
narrowly avoiding the ditch—
tomorrow morning, I'll find scratches
on the passenger door
from overgrown brush.

I feel like I'm still sixteen, driving with a permit,
seeing the Rocky Horror Picture Show for the first time,
cold morning, sitting on the floor next to the wood
stove—I can count on one hand
how many times I leave the house each week;
this is one of them—
still learning my own name.

I feel like I'm still nineteen, failing my first class,
isolated, again, this time on the ground floor—
discovering new ways to punish my body, surviving
anyway— learning, again, that we've always been
around, that community is more than your roommate
in undergrad.

I drive home with the high beams on—
I have to watch out for deer; I can't watch another
dying animal crawl into the brush,
not after that first hunting season—
hands numb, taking a bad shot, and dragging my body
out of the woods, holding the antlers

while my uncle saws through the skull.
Sometimes, I envy the deer.

The lights are on when I get home—
I smile, make conversation, ignore the panic
closing my throat—
I pretend to believe in something greater,
I shave, I pitch my voice up, I try to be
your daughter, and my performance isn't convincing.

I make my way upstairs—
tonight, I will sleep without air conditioning.
I'll fantasize about having my skin peeled away
and finding someone new underneath.

Among Your People *by Andre Zoolalian*

Lord,
if you sent an angel here,
would they need a gun?

Their accent would be foreign,
otherworldly,
their features like another species.

Their wings would drive envy,
and their eyes would breed lust.

They would walk the streets,
but would anyone walk with them?

Would they recognize your house
or would they look down in shame upon the pulpit?

Would they find our history
written in ink or in blood?

Lord, I know we need more angels,
but I'm not sure
we could handle one.

It's Not The Heat, It's The Housing *by Chelsey Reid*

"Can you help me with housing?" he asked.

As I lean out the side of the van the exhaust sears my
eyes that are already wrecked from the direct Kentucky
summer sun wafting up from the convenience store
parking lot like the dread of my knowing.

"Whatcha working on?" I reply gently, trying to soften
my honest response of, *"No."*

He explains the steps he's followed as instructed,
the deal with the city that included the fabled promise of
help if he'd just move somewhere more convenient for
concealment. He is not lazy, ardently chasing peace and
tomorrow by way of chance and change, practically
lassoing our van with bootstraps to seek The Resources.

But he is tired of waiting on waitlists that listlessly
ignore his calls. The log of attempts serving as a fancy,
inert paper trail documenting that someone somewhere is
trying to help with housing but excelling at collecting
paperweights.

He calls his buddies over, making sure they get what we
can offer. He's already excitedly selected for himself a
few pieces of candy and some snacks. His friend eyes a
specific flavor of taffy in his pile, and he smiles, swiftly
shoving the banana candy into the guy's palm.

What would it be like if we did a better job sharing what
we have, did a better job responsively noticing need and
desire? What if giving a damn and sharing were the
prescribed work requirements for those who *are* getting
by in this old world?

We ought to be on fire with shame, fuming like the mobile unit output and summer armpit asphalt, that housing, health, and food are luxuries, instead of gaslighting survival into indignity.

Driving home to my house, my clothes and body dripping with sweaty despair that I can wash away with a cool shower and a clean towel,

all I can do is marvel
at the humidity,
the humanity, and
the hypocrisy.

Sissies, Sluts, and Cereal Box Collectibles
by Ja'Quacy Kieron Minter

It's one of those days at the office where a morning cup of coffee paired with a burrito on payday isn't good enough. I need something with sustenance. I need today to be one of those days where life is nothing more than a bounce house castle and naivety. Instead, I'm sitting here at my desk—America's black sweetheart—sipping coffee—repetitively: mimicry. Back hurting—nails numb—feet swollen near the toes—yearning to make it to the other end of my nine-to-five. I miss my innocence. I miss the days when The Office was a cheesy, corny television show and not some somber reality.

Life was so simple then. You could drink water from the hose, piss alongside brick houses—whether you lived in them or not. You could walk the streets for hours unsupervised because the roads were safer, the
doors and windows were often open, and my classmates' chests existed without bullets: the good life. The safe life. A life cemented within simplicity. A time when small things like finding my favorite comic book or a funky figurine inside an old-fashioned cereal box made me happy. Hair nappy—neck smelly—belly full—body behaving like nothing more than a sissy—a slut. I wasn't America's black sweetheart then—no. I was just a slut in the making.

A sweet one at that—box after box after box of cereal—collecting—controlling—contorting–caught within the confines of fiber, corn, and oats—God, I miss my childhood.

I'm sitting at my desk, hurting, reminiscing, and missing the days when my biggest problem was finding the same figurine at the bottom of the barrel. Those days were so peculiar; gluttony was the norm then. Now, I hardly even have time to eat a full meal—only a few seconds for a spoonful or two here and there when I can. Speaking of remembrance, all I have felt lately is nostalgia—memory—moving ever so swiftly through me like electricity. Electric indeed—it stings—sights, savors, and symphonies have burned the portions of my body that carry the unwanted memories the most. The inner linings of my throat are sinched—my earlobes ablaze—my nostrils on fire, and my irises are festering. What is nostalgia, if not grief? What is grief if not a boy burning from the inside out?

When will it end? When will I stop hurting myself—burning myself—bent on bowls of memory? Collecting past figurines—seeking pleasure to find the boy within me—only to find pain instead. Memories bent on the bending over of my body—wanted or unwanted—to feel something, anything. Accepting blowjobs behind buildings in broad daylight to prove I can be a man—a king—of the jungle—of the bounce house—castles filled with quickies and hickeys from men I thought would love me when they only loved my body.

I was serving satisfaction—satisfactory—adolescence. I was moving too fast—too grown—too soon when I should have just been a kid. I was just a kid back then. Comic books, figurines, and old-fashioned cereal boxes should have satisfied me enough, and I wish I had known better. I wish I had known how to hold a man the right way before the night way—a slut. An abbreviation: seeking love under technicalities. Self-deprecation on repeat. Self-worth at the expense of self-destruction. Doing whatever for whoever to reach solubility.

Settlement. Satisfaction. Even now, I still settle. Even then, I walked the thin line between self-worth and solvency.

The more and more I write, the more and more I realize that I don't know how to love myself amid accountability. I want to hold myself accountable and remedy my mistakes through love, but it's hard. I'm hardheaded and stubborn; my time marinating in the wilderness has shown me this. It's shown me a lot about myself. It's shown me that I don't know how to love men beyond their bedrooms.

One encounter after another, I continuously collect them—box after box after box of cereal—collecting—controlling—contorting—caught within the confines of fiber, corn, and oats—a reflection. My reflection. I have become the man: hungry, howling, and eager. The slut in any article of clothing on any avenue at any given moment. Spread legs—mouth open—throat agape—ripe—ready—and hungry for the feeding.

But who could blame me? I was a sissy because the village that raised me was a woman. A slut because I learned to lust after men well before I knew how to love them. Be it by God or the men in my life, all I've ever known is servitude. I was always expected to serve. Bodies like this with hips like mine are served best by men and the dance floor. Serving looks as I vogue from one bedroom to the next. Libido at the limbo: a fast young man with even faster music—dancing with hips too grown—too fast—too soft—too sweet at fourteen. Blowing coaches—before kites, changing undies—before tires. I taught myself to ride like a lady, but I will never know how to ride a bike. I watched my body's kneecaps grow tender and change colors—purple looks good on me, I guess. I guess, as long as the sissies and the sluts are using their knees for Sunday's sermons, Saturday's sins don't matter. Beyond the bedroom, sissies and sluts like me don't matter. Serving cunt on Saturday, Christian on Sunday.

I want to be a man so bad. I want to know what masculinity tastes like—eager to understand my chest the same way I know my breasts—but I'm lost. I've spent so much time running from my past that I've accidentally run into women's clothing instead. I didn't know the man I was supposed to grow into. I still don't know him. I am still unknown. I still don't know how to ride a bike. I have never flown a kite or mastered the language of rubber—my palms don't know how to move tires from labor to reward. All I have known is pleasure—nothing else, and maybe that's the problem.

Maybe, just maybe, I don't know who I am because I am a conundrum of the men of my past. A melting pot of masculinity. Sitting here—after hours—alone at my desk, I yearned for more time.

There's a bowl of cereal in front of me as I sit here—pondering—wondering—collecting pieces of myself—poem after poem—working to recover the pieces of me that were collected by the hungry palms of man—bowl after bowl. Bite after bite. Spoonful after spoonful—caught—collected—and contorted within the confines of fiber, corn, and oats.

God, I miss my childhood.

Boys Like Me *by Eric Creech*

They told me boys like me don't get love
We get sick
They told me boys like me don't get love
We get shame

We get scorned and we get rejected
And we get pain
We are wrong and we are strange,
Boys like me

We get to creep silently and softly
And alone in the dark
We don't get to hold hands in the light
Or love unafraid

So boys like me grow up broken
And ashamed
Scared The truth will burn and expose
Boys like me

But here I am looking in the mirror at
a boy like me
Strong and whole and loved and free

A boy like me

compost part 1 and 2 *by Em Shepardson*

mist hugs the valley
of a blue skied island city
& I am sun kissed

pinky promising pines
I will be back soon
when their neighbor's
leaves grow gold

tomorrow
a gardener with
surgical precision
will harvest fruit
from my chest

my lungs will be
the first to know
we are free at last

---

if found, please return my trans body to the bluffs.
read each scar etched into my chest
it is a map of the Midwest. follow the Mississippi.
find the eagle's young &
lay me where the ghost pipes grow.
tell the trees I did my best.
& I'll tell the moon I am coming home.

On Time Loop Towns and Fifth-Generation Nobodies
by Rook Bell

And in the end, you're just a kid, shakin' and bitin' your lips until they're stained cherry red and pretendin' the blood ain't yours. Just a kid marchin' to the beat of the chant in your head—*chin up, lip stiff, don't let 'em see you cry.* So, in the end, you're just like everybody else here.

You can search this whole damn town, and I bet you won't find one kid that grew up with all the love they deserved. Nobody here makes it past fifteen without scars to show for it, and there's not a single person here that ever stopped bein' just a kid with too much weight to carry. In a place like this, it's predetermined. A town full of addicts and burnouts and wasted potential—it's a self-fulfillin' prophecy. If you wanna know where the kids will end up in a decade, just look at the parents. Most of 'em will stay right where they've always been, in the rundown houses and rusty pickup trucks they've shared with their siblings since they were sixteen.

It's not a lack of motivation. It's just that once you start a life somewhere, you get stuck, and the kids here have been workin' for years by the time they graduate, more often than not. And so they stay, and they tell themselves that when they're older they'll move away, drive off in the rusty old pickup, and never look back. But the years slip by, and they're still sixteen and too tired by the time they get off work to do anything but smoke and sleep.

Yeah, sure, they'd like to leave, but there ain't no point in wonderin' on things that'll never happen. Yeah, sure, they'd like to leave, but that takes money, and who's got that kind of money to spare? They're barely makin' rent as is. Yeah, sure, they'd like to leave, but that's a pipe dream, one they can't afford to indulge. The real world's always callin', and they best answer.

So, the cycle comes 'round again. They leave the leavin' to the kids—just like their parents left it to them.

Lightning Bugs *by Leo Coffey*

I don't see them bugs no more
flashing their little lanterns
as they shine like stars
                              dip
               pause
                                 fizzle out
I watch night sing to herself
the sun   too hot for sleeping
          her body at last   home
in barren creek beds
lay brittle fish skeletons   hungry
like waiting dogs
gone is that worn place   where
mythical fairy used to
dance   in total darkness
the same place I sliced my hand
on a muddy mason jar
trying to grab those bugs
              mid-flight
and keep them lit
                           forever

Between Butler and Roan Mountain
by Trish J. Gibson

There's a man-made lake called Watauga that stretches
out to the river, the Doe, the Elk, and just about
every other branch and creek in Carter County

Somewhere at the bottom of that 16-mile reservoir
are my sunglasses from two summers ago
when I got flipped off a float
and thought for just half a second
that I'd drowned

Last week I added my favorite hair clip
to that big underwater offering pile

I've heard that Watauga means "beautiful water"

But the Watauga is now filled with
giant branches and bottles
and who the hell knows what
else under the surface of the water

My sister-in-law asked why
there was so much debris this year

I yelled over the boat motor

"Helene"

Now I don't live here anymore
but I still know that there's trash from
where the water rose up on Roan Mountain
and when you're driving up
there are sections of road with no guardrail anymore

The rest of the country might have long forgotten
about Erwin, but none of us have

Insurance claims that don't cover natural disasters
and OSHA gave no citations
to Impact Plastics
after 5 employees were carried away

Those 5 people
were part of 251 total fatalities
from the storm that made its way up
the Blue Ridge Mountains

Meanwhile, everything and everyone
keeps moving

The graves have been covered,
local businesses have shuttered,
Hampton High School closed from damage,
and Poga Bridge got washed away

This year,
the deforestation of the state park has started
the local food bank was defunded
and only 8 months have passed
since that storm came

Too many other folks,
both in the South and far beyond
have intimately known this
kind of heartbreak, both long before
and since Helene

They've lost homes and lives to fires,
to floods,
to bombs,

to forced starvation,
and state violence

Each community will rebuild,
but so many will never recover

Here in Tennessee, the rhododendrons
are blooming up on Carver's Gap
even though the marked trail has been washed away

each year, the lightning bugs are fewer,
but still they're still synchronized and shining

Yes, Watauga Lake is full of branches,

and I'm here going for a swim.

Country Queens *by Jude DeWalt*

for Pauly Likens

There are bodies
scattered throughout these foothills.
At the bottom of Geneva swamp,
they are the foundation of the interstate.
They are lured out by corn feeders,
by older men disguised as lovers,
by raspberry bushes at the edges of properties.
Sharp, the thorns and the juice will stain you.
The youngest ones are found along French Creek,
limbs dotting the banks like road signs.

One summer, I maintained sewage lift stations,
learned grass stays growing,
up through the sidewalk cracks,
newly immune to last year's herbicide.
Dandelions come up regardless,
learning to grow shorter
with each pass of the mower,
until the flowers dodge the blade.
The leaves fall,
year after year after year,
mulching themselves into topsoil.
These things, which seem to grow
regardless of condition,
that plague your clean cut lawn and fertile field—
weeds are generous,
offering themselves up to you,
every time.

Carcass Pile *by Anna Hurd*

The deacons still insist that when they dig me up, I
will be her again. And in return
I don't bring up the carcass pile
at the bend, behind the pasture track.
I do not say
how far downstream I found myself that June,
how the bones were mixed, lips pulled away
from grinding teeth,
the multiflora rose pushed through the broken joints,
whether or not I wept. I do not tell them
anything about the benedictions I'd've given
to any such unhearing mound,
ankle-deep in clay, watching the rot for signs of life –
still can't say why,
and I don't say
that when they find my bones I will be seen, just once,
never again,
by an eight-year-old in cracking boots
who, she'll always think, did not expect me.

The Dirt Road *by Angel Ballew*

This is the place of fatherhood and of sisterhood,
the place of brotherly love and the fiercest mothering.
This is the Dirt Road, the ultimate *hood*.

The Dirt Road is a place of Communion,
where it's known that if you need something,
we'll provide it as a collective.
It's known if you're falling under the world's weight,
we will hold you.

This hood smells like honeysuckle and buttercups.
It feels like peace and tastes even sweeter,
like muscadines and blackberry pies,
like peaches and freedom all at once.

On my Dirt Road, honesty looks like facing our own
humanity, without fear or even shame.
It looks like embracing both our beauty and our
savagery. Here we sit in bold acceptance: we are both
predator and protector, made to destroy, to heal, and to
create something greater.

This is also where I was molded to work hard,
to grab what I want, who can tell me *no?*
I've got the grit and the means.
No weapon formed against me shall prosper.
If God is for me, who can be against me?
The world is mine, right?

But see, I think those words contain Southern Lies:
lies that tell me to rule and oversee,
lies that diminish the very peace I seek,
because how can power and community live
harmoniously?

Roots traveling down deep and new growth pushing
through, toward light, toward order.
Here I can worship Creation as just a creature
and not an overlord, 'cause Lord knows my control and
my order is destructive. Here I can garner, horde, and
share only the peace that sustains.

The whole of the road all feels like Grandma's glue,
you know, the *good stuff* that binds
that hug, or that wet-lip kiss.
Our hood feels like come get a plate,
rest yourself, be wild, uniquely you, and free—
but still somehow bound to one another

Here we learn that peace isn't really something to be
possessed, it is instead a state of being that we
collectively bring about. When we leave this road, we
leave renewed. I'll worship my own memories of this
place.

It is where God lives
and where my people are.

progress *by Josh May*

they whittled the hills.
three homesteads up this holler
folks gotta have a road
can't run their wagons
and surely not no automobile
through creekbeds forever.
what they didn't know
for each oak they chopped
well-water and mason-jars
lye soap and pickled hog's ears
persimmon pie and dulcimers
shed like snakehide.

A Wish, Our Wish *by Leigh Claire Schmidli*

When summer turned greenest, we gathered. We ate soft, mayo salads that stuck in our teeth. We told stories. You know how it is. *All* the stories.

We were children and grands, but we'd grown.

And the old folks wondered, "Where were the scraped knees? What happened to milkweed wishes? Caterpillars in pockets and leapfrog races?" We had none. We couldn't remember all the weeds made for wishing, and the swings—they only carried the wind off the lake.

Then one June, she was born—so small. We were tall. She grew half-inches. Her hair turned dark, long. Ours faded. The wind off the lake carried milkweed clouds, and we chased them—the sun bright on our faces. "Here," we said, giving her seeds. And with eager eyes, we followed her.

Her scrapes were our scrapes.
Every leap, our leap.
A wish, our wish.

But then she found her shape against the house. It had her outline and her doings.

"It never lets go of my feet," she said.

She'd only believed that the pine trees made shade—and the pick-ups and us. All the tall, taller things. But here it was, hers, drifting soft on the grass. It could move sharp and run. And as the sun traveled, high then low—her shade got tall. Long. Her reach grew, further and further, and away from us.

116

"Like a hill's," she said. "Like the trees'."

It's sad—how we closed our eyes to her then. We complained about the sun, how it angled, how bright on our faces. Silently, we wondered, Where *were* her scraped knees? What happened to milkweed wishes?

And with our eyes still clenched to the sun, we heard her say, "Here."

"Here."

The sun's heat left us, inch by inch. All complaints carried off—like seeds on the wind. That wind off the lake. We opened our eyes and saw what she'd become. A child, but growing, with roots buried deep. Real woody roots and elbows becoming branches now. Fingernails—leaves. She was catching the sun. Her shade washing over us.

Was this her wish? Our wish? A belief buried deep? Was it something dark or something bright? Or something simply untelling?

All we knew was they'd try to tell of it, try as they might.

"Like the hills," they'd say. When summers turn greenest, soft mayo salads stuck in their teeth.

They'd say, "She's the trees."

Good Mother *by Shaelyn Bishop*

I might have made a good mother
if we didn't burn methane gas,
if there were fewer of us, if we remembered
how to walk softly through the forests,
if there were still forests
if we hadn't erased the histories that mattered.

instead, I will implode
a smoldering, collapsing star.
I will flicker my light and send it out
for a million years, escaping
the gaping consumption of a black hole ending—
or is it beginning? I can never
remember.

I might have made a good mother
if I didn't wear my abuse around my body
like a cloak that slumps my shoulders,
if I hadn't been locked in that closet, if I didn't have
these scars, if I had never been given that drink.

instead, I will explode
a smoldering, glowing ember.
I will spit and fight and send out the spark
that sets all the trees alight
the roaring consumption of a landscape dying—
or is it rebirthing? I can never
remember.

maybe I would have made a good mother
if only this weren't and if only that were, if I wasn't
walking scar tissue, if the rivers still ran clean,
if I didn't hope to give something to the world
besides just another mouth, wanting.

so instead, I will disappear,
I will be the starlight fading,
I will be the fire burning down,
because if I want to be a good mother,
I must be the thread that runs out—
or is it unending? I can never
remember.

Hope in Threes *by Lexie Stepro*

The woman/stranger/Dee reminds us about the father,
the son, and the holy spirit outside the hospital.
A nine divided by three above the ICU door, a triple bypass,
three deer eating fruit in a yard.

My brother and I tell her that our mom loves elephants,
but only with the trunk up, for good luck. Lucky for us,
Dee knows about elephants with the trunk up.
Her person went in for surgery and the nurse
was wearing a scrub cap that had them all over.
That's how she knew God was there, of course.

Dee knows about signs—
us together, our meeting, is one.

Then there's Dean, too. He's always smoking
a cigarette right next to the "No Smoking" sign
when I walk outside to cry/ always making me feel
like a good daughter/ always saying
I'll know when it's time,

and then there's Debra, too. She's in her cartoon
cat shirt, waving through the tiny window
of their hospital room across the hall/ or walking past me
in our parking lot/ or sharing her table with me
over styrofoam boxes of hot food in our cafeteria.
Our wanting is so big it outweighs sadness.

Someone told me, "come boldly before God and tell him
what you need. He knows but he wants you to say it."
The whole time I'm watching the seasons change
in the open air chapel, I do more than say it.
I scream it. I cry it, real messy-like, and I never
quite find my way back into my body, but something

always walks me back through the hospital
to hold my mom's hand again.

She would make community here too,
with Dee/ and Dean/ and Debra.
I feel her in the way us strangers share the pain
and insist it gets easier to carry.

Kate Sits Next to Us at Thanksgiving
by Ellen Pauley Goff

We know what she says, us girls who grew
up when nothing tasted good enough
to crave anything but the flavor of empty,
sizes two and too small in our dreams of
what we might look like if we had a little
less above the waistline from those genes
working against us
(but the tv doesn't tell you that
if it can't sell you that).
After we've got big-girl money, these ingredients
become toxic and create model villains
who don't spend enough on clothes and protein.
Did you take your vitamins today?
Everyone should have been asking: who
made skinny feel good before the race began?
Grown-ups, we understand nothing rots
as fast as the girl who pinches herself
in front of the mirror, starving the idea
we could be better for the next young us.
But it's too easy to remember our moms
digesting their bodies in the same looking glass,
seeing fullness, mistaking presence for inconvenience,
so we realize we were doomed from the starting line.
Even when we think we're sugar-free of that girl
from thirteen and those repetitive hells of ritual,
do we ever shed that weight or do we layer and evolve
into creatures who better hide their weakness to survive?
Kate sits next to us at Thanksgiving and dishes
out the skinny: Beware,
the stomach can't ingest stress, ladies!
But if the enemy auctions the cure,
why would they ever thin the poison?
So we feed her the food news: There's this stunning

poem about radishes! It satiates the hunger
to devour someone's power, their skill with turning
torment into a moment of joy with a meal
of another time but at the same table.
See? we tell Kate. There is life after we diet,
we can outlive the men who ask for our minutes
but swear
they can't tell time with a curveless hourglass, who hate
they've now made us as flat and invincible as the boys
they once were.
That's good, Kate says, smiling over the biscuits
we will butter when we're alone.
Now the armor will fit better and this will hurt less.

The Hands of Time Have Liver Spots
by Emily Crenshaw

My grandaddy was a watchsmith.
He could make anything tick; my favorite
Was the clock in the kitchen with
A different bird's song chiming every hour.
There was a cardinal watching from his flower beds
The day my grandaddy left this house
For the very last time.

But before that, there was a time
When the red bird's song struck noon, and
We'd circle in the kitchen to bless the food—
Holding hands, spilling out into hallways—
A blessing so long the food got cold.
Bless this roof over our heads and bless
this home.

Long after our picture frames are gone,
Strangers' faces in their places,
These walls remember a cacophony of voices.
Accents always thicker here,
Not like honey or molasses
But like getting stuck in the mud.
The tread on our tires worn from our time away,
Unpracticed, spinning our wheels until we find purchase
And our voices slow
And our vowels drag
Like we never left.

Nostalgia's fickle and time's a thief—
I'd love to swap those days for all this grief
And walk into my grandparents' house again.

Eat wild sculpins off the vine,
Hug their necks with no thoughts of time
And feel the breeze like feathers on my skin.

See them waving in the carport side by side
Then fall asleep halfway through the drive,
Too young to realize they're growing old.

Seeds as Testament *by Amy Le Ann Richardson*
for the women with dirt beneath their nails

I didn't inherit land
so much as a way of being on it
barefoot in garden rows,
shoulders burnt,
quiet with the knowing
that comes from watching
something grow,
because you stayed.

I was raised on a hillside that leaned
just enough to test your balance.
We planted tomatoes in the strip
Papaw cleared with his own breath
lungs gone soft from cigarettes
and peppermints passed like heirlooms.

Every woman in my bloodline
knew how to stretch meat,
mend silence,
wrap grief in beeswax and twine.
They didn't write books,
but they taught me how to
read a sky before it breaks.

Just hands
in dough,
in dirt,
in hair braided before school.
They sang while they kneaded,
left stories pressed into flour
like fingerprints on a mason jar.

Their stories came out
in what they fed us
green beans put up in September,
songs hummed while canning
to keep the heat from being heavy,
grief folded into biscuits.

I've carried their names like seeds
tucked into the hem of my coat
not to be sown all at once,
but saved.

For when the world forgets
that we were ever here.

Now I carry them
in a worn notebook,
in poems I read aloud
to women who've forgotten they have voices.
I tell them: the stories are still here.

We are still here.

Power tried to silence us,
but we know how to speak in seeds.

I stand in fields
where corn has failed and started again.
I write poems from calluses,
pray over compost.

The land doesn't forget who listens.

I've seen a room change
when a woman finds her own story
in another's voice.

That shift—that yes, I remember, too—
it's what I plant now.
It's what I leave behind.

And when they come for our stories,
and they will,
I'll be ready
with a spade
and a stack of stitched journals.

I'll open my hands
and show them
what we saved.

Old Woman: And Everything She Passed Down
by Lucas Evelyn Poynter

May I never forget the way she said "juice"
with a "d" at the end—"joost,"
like the word got stuck in her teeth.

May I never forget the rows of green beans, tomatoes,
and sunflowers taller than us kids in the garden,
leaving bug bites and scratches
as we fought through weeds
to fill our plastic buckets,
the trampoline that left our skin hot and sticky,
and the wooden playhouse that was
splintered as if it didn't want to be played in.

May I remember passing around the cloudy
jug of water from her fridge,
where it was sweating on the top shelf
beside the pickled eggs and waxy slices of bologna,
beads of condensation slicking the plastic,
with its handle that was always a little sticky.

I'm still looking for something as soul-quenching as that.

May I remember the fan on my face
as I basked on her loveseat,
lulled to sleep in the afternoon heat,
shutting my eyes to our crooked-ass faces on her walls.
No art, just us. '80s prom portraits and chubby babies
with frosting still on their cheeks.

May I still hear the singings on the TV in the kitchen
and the ones in the barns down Conway.
May I return to the games of rummy with Rojo and Bev,
for I know they've been waiting for me to take my turn,

and may I have tonight just one more talk with her—
about anything—the weather, God, her
disappointment in who I have become.
Anything.

I have to believe that, in another life,
we'd still have each other.
She'd be bopping around Berea
in her PT Cruiser,
complaining that there is nothing to do
now that all the singing barns are closed
and all her friends are dead.
I'd be calling her *old woman.*
She'd flash that ornery grin and say, *"Now, Laney..."*

But that's a story for another day,
and this is the eulogy I should've written
a long time ago.

Part of me still believes that the good in me is all her.
I know that it's been long enough that it can't be,
but Mammaw laid my foundation.
She showed me who to look out for—
those folks who've got a little bit of Evelyn in them.
I know to keep them around.

Now, all I've got left of her are
my memories, her voice in my head,
her red hair in my beard, and a little
sailboat magnet that made it all the way
from her fridge to mine.

Old woman, if you can hear me,
I'm holding on tight.

The Creeks Speak *by Mecca Collins*

The creeks speak to me,
its whispers trickle down
my ear canal. The
creeks breathe shallow breaths,
cool and slow. from
within the hollers, they
holler muffled watery
calls into the trees, and I am beckoned nearer
to their partially clear
bodies. Skipping rocks,
no socks, in the midst of the Big Wheeling.
A feeling unmatched when I hear the creeks speak,
and I listen. They call out my name,
It ricochets across the vast West Virginia eminence.

Home is the Place Where, When You Go There, You Only Think About How to Get Out *by Pauletta Hansel*

Busted-up doll heads where the canned goods used to be.
Sun-steeped, hillbuckled sidewalks, and everybody
just looks tired. Nobody cares
this is where your mother used to buy her meat.
The houses you lived in plowed under,
moles scuttle through plumbing cracked
with black dirt and roots.
Nobody cares about your old woman body
grown on the bones of the girl who walked these streets.
Everybody has their own worn bones.
Everybody remembers you, sort of.
The newspaperman calls you by your mother's name.
You can't remember the name
of who you sat next to in math class or whose backseat
you crawled out of nights, the river fog
so dense you came home hair and misplaced clothes
all damp and smelling like mountain. Nobody cares
you know this town by what is gone, stench
of grease spilled from the closed pool hall,
mailbox on the corner
where the boys sprawled, pelvises jutted out
to block your path.
You pull up your car too close to the high curb
somebody told you was made for hitching horses.
Nobody had any horses.

Previously published in Heartbreak Tree (Madville Publishing, 2022)

Hillbillies Need No Elegy *by Beth Wolfe*
*with respect to The Bitter Southerner General Store for
the title*

I sing no elegy for the timeworn hills that cradled and
protected the dreams of all I could do or be,
an unshakeable foundation where I stood
and looked out to a future some in the world
wanted to deny me.

I sing no elegy for the constant rivers running through
my childhood, crisscrossed with bridges carrying me to
those I loved time and again; rivers both calm and wild,
still carving and creating, showing us how to keep
moving forward.

I sing no elegy for the sky that stretched beyond our
imaginations and blanketed our summer nights, when we
chased each other and our futures, wondering if that sky
looked any different in the places we'd never been.

I sing no elegy for those who have gone on to worlds
beyond, their voices still ringing full of wisdom in my
ears, their love abiding within my very bones.

I sing no elegy for those of us still here, striving to make
a way for ourselves, our neighbors, our children and our
students—still knowing the power of being kind to a
stranger, still trusting there is more good than evil in the
world, and still believing there is more to life than
climbing the proverbial ladder and worshipping the
almighty dollar.

I sing no elegy for all of us who know the comfort of a
hand-sewn quilt, the magic of a Mason jar full of
lightnin' bugs, and the soaring beauty of four-part

harmony on a Sunday morning; for those who've lived
the experience of pinto beans and cornbread filling more
than a hungry stomach, and who believe in lifting each
other up rather than tearing each other down.

We are not lost, we are not dead.

I sing of our spirit, our determination.
I sing of our contributions, creations, and discoveries.
I sing of our home, our beautiful,
almost heaven home.
And I sing of who we were, and are,
And will someday be.

I sing us no elegy.

Progress *by Rook Bell*

Then came the developers, those industry men,
with their CATs and cranes and their little worker ants
marching two by two.

They came with their jagged metal hands, reaching into
the heart of this place and hollowing it out,
to fill it with their thick grey sludge and promises of
progress, and they did not ask permission.

And they did not need it. And we did not ask for
them or their progress, but we understand it is not us
they build for.

My grandmother points to the Kroger store that, as far as
I'm concerned, has always been there,
points and says *I remember when there were cows there.*
The field of trees and wildflowers between the big
church and the car lot has given way to
pavement and rubble and busy yellow machines that
cannot make up for the dandelions they stole.
The gutted convenience store on Broadway now houses
a shiny new bar in its once-empty belly.

Their *progress* creeps, not like rot—that's home, that's
home—but like a spreading bleach stain.

In April I stay in, and when I emerge from my hovel in
May the old pawn shop on Main has been swallowed
by an artisan ice cream joint and its plus-one,
a Southern-chic boutique selling clothes we don't want,
and couldn't afford if we did,
buzzing with artsy 30-somethings with sunglasses and
wine glasses and faces I don't recognize.

Every drive we take around town now,
there's a new lot levelled,
always for storage units or a car wash,
or a new suburban maze of towering identical houses
we would never be allowed inside,
and not even the roads look the same anymore.
All the rusty little pickups are dying off,
hulking replicas springing up in their place,
always bigger, brighter, taller, louder,
and with never a speck of mud on their glistening,
untouched flanks.

And each time we drive by their cars,
them playing pretend at a blue-collar life,
or their expanses of broken land,
cut up and parcelled out,
we shake our heads or roll our eyes,
mutter curses or heave a sigh,
but at the end of the day
we just return home and wonder
what will be the next to go.

This place has always been part graveyard, part
battleground, but wholly ours.
I've loved and hated it in unequal measure. In my
desperate moments, I've dreamt of it, in turns,
          burning or being reborn.
But in every image of revenge or reformation
I've clutched to my chest, the landscape has been
the one I still recognize.
In my mind, this place has always been
separate and untouchable.
Cruel and stifling and rotting, yes,
but safe, at least, from the ever-march onward of the
world beyond the county line.

Now, its face is almost unknown to me.

I always dreamt of leaving, but I never imagined
there would be nothing left of this place that
           birthed me to leave behind.
I wonder now if, by the time my wounds
—shaped by a childhood in this town—
heal shut, there will be anything left
to receive my forgiveness.

The Overspill *by Leo Coffey*

The river carved itself
a new path where
Running Ridge Road used to be
there's cars sitting belly up
gutted by the river's current
  across Asheville
buzzards fly overhead
and forage for bodies
scour oak trees for limbs
  on the news
an old man talks about
his garden
once swarmed
with rhododendron
where he found a child wrapped in
pink pajamas   blue
her face   her body
soft and cold
neighbors say she
floated the French Broad
amidst debris and
rainbow trout
the old man says he wonders
how fast he'll need to swim
next time water rises
  and there ain't
    no higher ground

After the War: Part I *by christa kaodi*

After the war…

When the children
Return to the classroom
(which is no longer a classroom)
But stories of debris
(both natural and artificial)
A neat row of blankets
(which now are prayer mats)
A collection of little souls
(which once had full houses)

Float, grounded
On tepid water
Ankles cooling, somehow,
While, somewhere,
The ocean boils.

The women
(who have always been the libraries)
Have now become
The curriculum
The course catalogue
The text book.

Chapter one: What we were before the war
Chapter two: The war.
Chapter three: What we will become after the war
Chapter four: When the war is won

My children,
My collection of souls—

Everything that was, is
Now held lovingly,

Guarded by my skin,
Brown as all natural debris and
Twice as useful,
Three times as storied

Everything that was
Comes back home
In a mother tongue.

The mothers
Our conduit
Our library
Our canon

After the war…

The author has noted this piece is to be read slowly, with measure, in a silent environment

To Preston *by Jovan Mays*
Commission for the Equal Justice Initiative in
conjunction with the National Lynching Museum

Sometimes I wonder,
at what age do we know our songs?
At what time do our bodies become our melodies, our
cadences, our chords?
I can still hear my grandma humming a
melody into a meal.
I wonder what your dad sang, Preston, to trick you and
your brother's hunger into bedtime,
to trick the house into cradling itself to sleep.

Yeah, sometimes I wonder,
I wonder if we all have the same fascinations of fire.
Lord knows you must not.
The act of putting a fresh log into a stove and watching
the house cradle itself to sleep.

Did you ever wonder where embers go?
Have you imagined their return to the sun?
I hope you did, Preston.
A star ain't nothing but a fire.

You know I have gathered lumber for long winters,
and I know you know such work—
how to get into a log-hurling rhythm,
how to trick up the speed to stack fast.

They call a full bed of firewood a chord,
and four full chords should get you through the winter.
But, there's those chords again—
did you get to know your song, Preston?

They say, in music, a chord is a harmony of three notes,

and I think about you, signing the pages of the Gospel of
Luke and handing them to your future executioners.
And how they used those as invitations to your concert,

your solo on the stake,
your terror on that tie,
the cadence of your chains,
the choral of your kerosene,
accenting a symphony of splinters,
as your throat became their justice.
Do you think they heard you, Preston?

Did they register the register of your wails, your
weeping? Did they, Preston?
Did they hear your family in your lungs?
Did they see your human as your skin molted?
Did they catch the signals in your smoke?

On the Eastern Plains of Colorado,
the wind can be spellbinding.
Some say it can even sweep,
and Lord, how we saw them sweep you, Preston,
under our flagged rug, swept your remains
so that you would not.

But, I think of a sweep, Preston,
how it can be lifting,
how it can carry you when you can't carry yourself.

Oh, I know wind.
Out here in these plains,
they farm wind to recharge.
Turnbinded, they watch their houses
cradle themselves to sleep.

And at night, when it's just you and the moon,

if you listen real deep, you'll hear the wind howl.

They say that wolves wail to the sky to call the pack,
and what else is a howl but a song?
Calling us in, to a choir of chords
bottled in confession and confusion,
teenaged and tormented,
wondering if it was ever heard.

But somewhere,
under all that brimstone,
under all that char,
in that Holocaust combustion,
was a song
constructed by a Preston Porter Jr.

We say your name,
we play your chords,
every time we hear this wind
on the Eastern Plains,
calling us in, reminding us,
that we have some songs to teach.

On November 16, 1900, a 15-year-old Black teenager named Preston "John" Porter Jr. was burned alive while chained to a railroad stake in Limon, Colorado. A mob of more than 300 white people from throughout Lincoln County gathered to participate in the brutal public spectacle lynching.

For You *by Thailan Franklin*

What is it like to be free? To be able to contort
yourself—not the contortion of forcing your body to fit
someone else's standards, but contortion as privilege, as
power, as opportunity. Contortion: to twist and bend
however you please.

Freedom doesn't feel free to me.

It feels like lower-back pain at 23 from standing on
warehouse concrete, like "veggie stir-fry" for lunch.
Heavy as owing the IRS. Heavy as being the first college
graduate in your family without the capital to cross the
finish line.

Freedom feels like the time I choked in a Target parking
lot—when I'd never been that close to losing my life, or
so I thought. It feels like almost losing your life. It feels
like your mama slapping her palm on your back as hard
as she can, all too familiar with the hard candy lodged in
your throat. Freedom feels like her fear.

Freedom feels like watching your mama notice you
struggle and having no freedom to do anything about it.
It feels like generational trauma: hiding in your body,
showing up as Sunday-morning sweeping and
Sunday-night mourning. A bed caved under the weight
of your "freedom," the deepest indentation where your
shoulders and chest lie.

Freedom feels like not knowing whether you're
neurodivergent or lazy. Or just Black. Or just a woman.
Or just a Black woman. It feels like a gender binary—no
matter how many titty-lifting tops you wear or how
many loose, thrifted men's button-downs you buy,
they'll still force you to pick between two.

Freedom feels like being a spiritual being obliged to embodiment in a physical world, forced into their charades.

Freedom is unrelenting.

You don't know if it exists. You thought, briefly, that it did, but that feeling wasn't freedom. It was deception masking itself as such: a drug, like LSD, tinting the world bright and letting you invent new shapes with your eyes. That deception is addicting. They feed it to you to make you chase long desires with temporary fixes. They feed you false comforts to keep you weak, to worsen your lower-back pain, to tell you vegetables are enough, to say paying taxes buys you care, to whisper that college isn't for you, to make candy a warning and your mother's fear your own.

The temporary fix tells you you're lazy, that you're merely a woman, that the charades are real.

The facades shout:
Freedom does not exist for you.

Removal Act *by Charlotte Isenberg*

for a cruel moment, I saw you:
flicker of firefly.

among Jesusland you stood,
watching,
as I fell,
screaming,
to that ivory,
blinding and bitter.

my antlers danced,
a fearsome shadow
foreign and dear.

the dogs barked.
I was clean,
carved legs caught on the leather,
in black bars and southern night.

I looked through
to my angel,
trap-caught and white as a scar,
then touched my stomach and sighed.

I slumped onto you.
"is this what it is,
to be an Indian woman?"
I asked.

"I cannot say,
just guess,
for I know only a broken heap of images."

your laugh chimed in the air,
thinned the distance.

"woman"
you chided,
"if they had called you Indian,
you would not have been so lucky."

I laughed at you laughing at me,
hand in hand,
half of your half.

I told you I love you,
looking up into the black sky.
you told me it is all we have.

Valley of the Sun *by Idris Isaiah Irihamye*

The sun is resting behind snow-filled clouds
        while the decomposers in the humus do
        their honorable work,
                and I do mine.
The only thing I can give the winter is my warmth.
Look at me, I trail after love
        like an altar server after the priest.

See, if my fate is exile or a life in the tower,
        I will run every time, you know this.
And they will call me a wild thing, and I will scowl
        and they will see my serpentine skin
        and know that they will never catch me.
They don't even understand yet,
        how easy I've made this for them.
How I've taken the sharp teeth out of my wolf's mouth
        and made myself an herbivore.

Move to the mountains with me.
There's a township named after you along a creek
        called Hell For Certain. You can interrupt my
        sweeping with a kiss.
You know, I sat still reading for so long once,
        that a spider wove me into its silk highway
        network, like I was the mountain I-64 winds
        around.

Maybe one day, I'll finally weave a prophecy
        where my truth makes my love mine.

Silvers *by Cassie Andresen*

Everyone drilled into us that marriage would be
the most Herculean of all our labors
and yet
it may be the most effortless thing
I've ever done.

My wife and I experience dreadful exasperation
whenever we hear individuals whine or fuss
over their respective spouse
which has only been exacerbated
by the many years and tears of
traditionalist relatives and crimson senators
Threatening our liberty to love
and to my dream honeymoon suite
that was located beside my bride's hospital bed
during her six day emergency Harborview stay.

So when I hear a man make a crack
at his life partner's weight
at the miracle of her body
When I hear a woman complain to her sisters
of how her other half never puts his dishes in the sink,
laundry be damned
When I hear the phrase "marriage is just so hard,"
or often "we've been through our highs and lows,"
or even "sometimes I just want to wring his neck..."
or

When I hear a husband,
this bastard who's already been blessed
with a decade of marriage to his wife,
glamorize, romanticize, fantasize
an affair with some woman
whose skin is more supple

knees more knobby
instinct less developed
a doe with a few white spots still left on her back
I am filled with a rage so fiery it finally makes sense
why I was born a month early
at March's close.

I'd give each limb away to any God
one by one
if it meant we'd be promised
just a bit more time
to watch her silvers come in
Moonstories written from her scalp
Salt and pepper constellations
draping down her back.

This existential hell we've learned to make a home of
has rooted my heels so deep into my earthen humanity
I struggle to see much beauty in youth anymore
My mind, body, and soul fail to comprehend
this societal obsession with adolescence
With the infatuation of appearing younger
than you are
than you get to be.
I am instead fawning over
the oxygen-snatching sex appeal
Of her first grey hair
Of the crinkles deepening around her eyes
every time she laughs at a cancer joke
because what else is there to do at this point?

Whoever thinks thirty is old must not grasp
the staggering attraction of
Sunspots
A forehead with a memoir
Hair so pearly one could only assume

Aphrodite made love to them in her oyster.
I ache to see her tattoos wrinkle,
fading deeper into the skin
night by night
almost as if they were embedded there
prior to her cesarean extraction.
I am wet when I imagine her birthday candles
Hard when I picture wooden rocking chairs
on a rusted front porch
Melting whenever I learn we get the privilege of living
a little more life together.
I'll never need another hit
if I get to wake up next to her
one more morning.

Love cannot be taken for granted
Years, we found out, are not offered lightly
Not when tumors like this exist.

My love to my lover is
Hope in its simplest form
encased in custom warmth
A romance so generative there is no choice
but to express it with my whole chest
A family so obvious, blood is not necessary
A swelling
A lifeline
The reason
My name on her lips at 2am
on a barren sidewalk or in our blue velvet bed
The scar on her knee, a spiritual reckoning
A foundation of intuition layered in trust
A garden blooming in my ribs
when she sings Counting Crows in the shower
The word "Why?"

at the end of the 12 minute live track,
an atheist prayer to the contrast of white on white
Euphoria in the lowlight
Boredom learning to fly
My baby cousin falling asleep
to her singing voice and pendulum arms
in a rickety campsite
The honor of making her chamomile tea at 8:45pm.

To my wife,
today my gratitude for the universe
comes in the form of an early silver strand
I watched glisten on your pillow last night
One that cast over the corner of your eyelid
falling down to frame your face.
It was a gift from our galaxies,
the nebulas that age beyond
what we could ever humanly appreciate
Just as you have, my love.
With every offering, I am given yet another addition
to my exponential purpose of worshiping at your altar
All the brilliance and beauty of you
You and your moonbeam mind
You and your lavender honey heart.

Labor of Love *by Emily Crenshaw*

I was passed down
My grandmother's ring
And my grandmother's rage
That I will spit and spew for her
After all those years
They made her swallow it.

From this day forward,
Her diamond weighs on my ring finger,
A promise to make the choices she never had—
To love and to cherish
Myself first always,
For better or for worse.

For richer or for poorer,
I'll have a tank full of gas
And a sock stuffed with cash;
I'll never love without an exit plan.
With all that I am
And all that I have,
This is my solemn vow:
I'll never be a ghost in my own home before I'm gone.

Plant Management *by Elizabeth Roach-Smith*

I speak to plants like a snake charmer,
Soothing, guiding, lulling,
My bright mottled babies,
Neatly arranged
Like desks in a classroom,
But as they grow,
They spill out of the rows like slouching teenagers,
Mildly rebellious,
Flaunting their growth,
With their spreading, decadent leaves,
They may sass me at times,
But occasionally listen.

Vegetable-tending winds
Through my bloodline
Like tobacco vines,
Or the slithering racerbacks
That warm their bellies
On the luscious brown earth,
Peeking out shyly as debutantes
From beneath leafy verdant shelters,
That protect their delicate complexions
From the sun,
And from inscrutable characters like me,
Often benevolent,
Occasionally antagonist,
When we're at crossways,
Grudging neighbors that can turn vicious.

I mostly have the upper hand,
Except when I don't.

Rotting rhubarb,
Beetle-ridden blackberries,

Sun-parched corn,
Rain-soaked greens,
Frostbitten strawberries,

Yet,

Today, summer sunshine warms my back,
A soft breeze rustles my hair,
As a sparrow bids me good morning,
Curiously eyeing me,
Biscuits and bacon await me at the kitchen table,
Along with fresh-sliced tomatoes,
The juices drizzling into my sunflower-yellow eggs,
No longer a seedling to be raised,
But the mature fruit of my teachings,
Taking its turn to mother me,
Nourishing and forgiving.

How You Do It by *Alicia Wright*

I. Fists full of mud on Sunday morning,
heels sunk deep in effluent washed
to the valley floor. Narrow stream-

furrow cuts the field, hooks
around a stranded cohosh.

II. Shovel swung sure in the glossy dark
hacks at sponge-soft ground. The high moon
paints the dogwood bright,
paints the water nickel-green, shines it still
as a mirror in the catchment behind the trees.

III. Blister splits thumb web to salt
a riverine palm. Even worn tools
kiss back.

IV. Spigot through concrete, knuckles
scrubbed raw in brass and lime—

pull it by the willowy neck, yank
roots shaggy into the purpling sky—

V. It comes back stranger: a racket,
a low rumble. It remembers its shape,
remembers the name of the bruise.

Ode to Mother *by Jessica Powers*

Woman with too many dogs   Woman who fantasizes
about winning the lottery: she will pay off the house
she will buy all us kids a house   she will build
brand new house   out of bone and dirt   she will
keep creek / pool / barn / bridge / long gravel driveway
woman who says *you'll have to carry me out of this
house in a box*   she will take us all on a European
vacation: Italy / Ireland / Scotland / France / Greece
everywhere we are supposedly from   Woman with
too many wants   with long, raven-curled hair
Woman I came from   Woman who prays   on the
broken bridge   how I love her daydreams
Woman with too many impulses but I don't care
let's spend too much money at the thrift store because
we are together and delusional   Woman waiting for
something good to happen   or just summer
Woman with a messy house   and men that don't
clean   Woman trying to spin animal fur into
gold   land into livelihood   Woman fantasizing
future   and I am right there with her
delightful delusions on a Sunday   Women always
aching for home

Raised Voices *by Cassidy White & Kelli Claypool White*

Kelli (Mother):
To get to the end, I have to start at the beginning. It's 1968, small-town Kentucky. A square bordered by family shops, with a courthouse anchoring the center. My parents welcome a 5 lb. 7 oz. baby girl into the world.

I had a peaceful childhood: no raised voices, no violence, just playing outside until dark, afraid of werewolves instead of people. My parents gifted me that. And maybe that's why I was so unprepared for what came next.

In 1983, at fifteen, I met him. I didn't know then how one day can lead to a lifetime of others. He was older. Soon, we were exclusive. And, quickly, romance became control. Pep rallies spent alone in the library. No makeup. Phone calls upon waking and before bed. Surveillance disguised as love. Compliance framed as protection. But from what? From whom?

It took me years to admit: I needed protection from him—and from myself. From shame, pride, and the belief that my worth had diminished. I judged myself harshly. Now, I look at teenage girls and think: I would never judge them the way I judged myself. I would love them, help them, protect them.

Cassidy (Daughter):
As a child, I escaped through books. Reading was the one thing that quieted my anxiety, and later, it gave me something even more essential—language. When I finally found the vocabulary for what had happened in our home, it changed me.
I used to think I'd never end up with an angry

man—but the truth is, I *was* the angry man. I held so much rage. My father was paranoid, dangerous, cruel. I feared for my life, yes—but what burned hottest was watching what he did to my mother. That's the fire I still carry.

In college, I found a story by Catherine Lacey—about a woman with a mysterious "crotch wound" (oh, how I love women). It wasn't the wound that stuck with me. It was a poem written by a student in the story:

> "if you're raised with an angry man in your house,/ there will always be an angry man in your house./ you will find him even when he is not there./ and if one day you find that there is/ no angry man in your house—well, you will go find one and invite him in!"

I didn't invite him in. He was already inside of me. That rage was the only thing that made me feel safe, feel seen. My rage was—is—justified. I was her witness. I needed people to see her. To see me. But violence silences you. And silence, over time, becomes its own form of violence.

Kelli:
I married him. We were together for 33 years. And he gave me the three most radiant souls I have ever known. Would I change everything to avoid the heartbreak and the violence? Yes. And no. Because those children—they are my restoration.

But still, I hope they can forgive all I didn't know. They grew up in the same small town I did, but without the same silence. They heard the yelling. They saw the bruises, physical and not. And still, they shine. They are stronger and more resilient than I ever hoped to be.

Cassidy:
Our lives were shaped by silence. Now, we get to
be loud. Even boisterous. Side by side.

I'm not the angry man anymore. I'm a woman who
loves, who laughs with friends, who walks her sweet
dog, Ms. Liz, and sips orange wine and reads until her
eyes blur. Who tends to her rage like a guest on the
front porch—and then lets it go home.

We are not ashamed of what we lived through. Rage is
not something we hide from anymore—it was righteous,
and it came from love. Love for ourselves, for each
other, for the girls we used to be. My mother says she
would never judge a teenage girl for what she didn't yet
know—and I wouldn't judge my mother, either, for
what she had to survive. Even in the worst moments,
there were still soft ones. Quiet joys. Small freedoms.

And now, there's this: the courage to name what
happened. To write it down. To be seen. Because it
matters that we speak. It matters more than anyone
ever told us.

Grouse Cover *by Anna Hurd*

I don't hunt. But
when I drive, the part of me
that's from my father sinks its boot onto the brakes
at a glimpse of grouse cover: reaction
to abundance,
an eden on the other side
of every ditch.
Rolling past the tangled laden vines I am
for a beat, all clay:
now packed tight and heavy,
waterlogged—now,
just as sudden,
all dug up.

Appalachian Anthem *by Beth Wolfe*
after "Declaration" by Lizzie Wann

This is a challenge to the big city know-it-alls.

This is what you don't know
because you didn't make a leaf notebook in your
sixth-grade science class.

This is what you missed
because the stars in your sky
aren't stars but lights
from impossibly tall buildings.

This is the sound of the tiniest pieces of gravel crunching
beneath the tires of our cars—
a sound you'd never hear amidst the furious honking of
impatient, angry drivers.

This is a window into our hearts—
ones you refuse to understand because your feelings of
superiority comfort you, attempting to fill a hole you
don't know the source of,
leaving you gaping nonetheless.

This is my anthem—one I sing boldly—the one you will
hear but cannot know.

The Ring Fits the Same *by Bradley Firchow*

People who've never been here always ask the same
thing.

*Morehead? Like the university? Isn't that where Kim
Davis raised hell?*

They mean well. But they miss the point.

What they know about this place is often what made the
news.

And what made the news barely eclipses the truth.

The truth is this: the hills cradle us. They fold around
this little town like a grandmother's quilt, pulled up in
the night, stitched with redbud and creek rock, moss and
memory. The light comes gentle in the mornings, lifting
fog from the tops of the sycamores. There's a rhythm
here, not always easy, but always alive.

Two men live in an apartment above Main Street.
They're not from here, not exactly, but they've made a
home. Married just over a year. They bicker about dinner
and wrap their arms around each other in the dark. A
terrier is curled up on the couch, gnawing on an antler
and twitching in his sleep. There's a gold ring on one
man's hand, passed down from his grandfather's 62
years of marriage — scuffed, imperfect, beloved. An
honest inheritance.

In the evenings, they walk straight from their front door
into the forest. They speak the names of wildflowers like
blessings. Dig in garden beds. Brew kombucha in the
closet and knead bread with hands that remember the

163

work of generations. They pick blackberries in summer. Their boots carry dust from the trail and flour from the kitchen.

This is what queer life looks like in the hills. Not spectacle, not tragedy. Just living. Just *being*.

And they are not alone.

There's the retired doctor and her wife who grow enough squash and beans to feed half the county. A quiet couple that still walks their mule along the fence line, reading poetry aloud between the posts. The trans elder who never found her way to hormones but learned, in time, to love the body that carried her through. A bartender. A pastor's daughter. A poet. A social worker who goes home to his husband of fifteen years, porchlight always left on.

The lives we live are seldom loud. They don't often make it past the county line. But they are sacred. They are whole.

Kingsolver once wrote, "The very least you can do in your life is figure out what you hope for. And the most you can do is live inside that hope."

That's what we do here. We live inside hope like it's a house with creaking floors and sun-warmed windows. We hang our laundry in it. We light stoves and tend gardens and hold each other through storms.

There is history here — some of it painful, some of it holy. There is memory and inheritance and the long work of healing. And yes, Kim Davis might make headlines again this summer. But in the meantime, we

are planting tomatoes. Hosting potlucks. Making love.
Frying potatoes in bacon grease. Lighting candles.
Writing poems. Showing up.

Creation, in the face of erasure, *is* a way forward. A way
to name ourselves without apology. A way to take up
space in the hollers and on the hilltops, on gravel roads
and courthouse steps.

We do not need to be exceptional to belong.

We already do.

And the hills, tough and tender, know our names.

Corpse Bird *by Audrey Nidiffer*

Meatloaf burns the smell of sage through Bobbie's house
Green beans boil while mashed potatoes bubble
Products of the Appalachian Food Machine
That rises up every time the death bell tolls

Aunt Jill brought the meatloaf and wine
I brought Boar's head sandwiches
Karen who used to own the flower shop
Brought casserole

That's just how we grieve

The sky turns a rose pink before creeping back
Over the valley line
Drawing a brown shadow across the kitchen table
As I write my cousin's obituary
That's what the Angel of death told my family
My english degree is worth
Writing family obituaries so I can practice
Until it's time to write my mother's
Like she wrote her father's

Momma watches over my shoulder
Eyes heavy with tears that have continually cascaded
For the past four years

That's just how we grieve

At the altar on All Saints Sunday
She read the names written in sharpie
On the white tablecloth

Lonnie, Poppy, Granny, Joel

And asked
"Who's next?"

That's just how we grieve

As we pass slices of meatloaf around
Bobbie says Lance woke her up last night
She felt his hand on her shoulder and that's how
she knew he was gone
A week after Poppy died Momma said he'd told her
"You can't come where I am right now"

Jill says she knew her grandmother was gonna die
Under a blue September sky just by a feeling

That's just how we grieve

Maybe it's retrospect the act of traveling back in grief
But my mom hovers her hand by my temple
"You're as heavy as Bobbie is,
what do you need to let go?"
And I tell her how on the drive home from the hospital
Just before she called to tell me Lance had died
The corpse bird flew gray
Right over my windshield and I knew
She just nodded

Flower Crown *by Kelsey Voit*

In December, I
walked the creek meadow,
where a mama cow
died this spring—
something wrong with her gut.
I saw
her scattered
bones
laid to rest.
Hips, femur,
half a jaw with
teeth intact
in the soft new green of
where the sun
kissed the frost away.
Brown stems held their ruptured breath
where ice flowers burst,
freeze forcing
death until spring,
then death again.
Fragile ice sheets
of croissant, of rainbow,
push from earth and stem
to layer into delicate,
swooping brush strokes—each a
fleeting flower,
a stage for sugar plum fairies
to dance upon the heifer's crystal crown.
Amidst death and dance,
I burst into joy,
witness to gratitude.

Aunt Tennessee: An Ode to Folk Magic
by Susanna Spearman

you were a bird-skeleton crackle
what kind of drum, your mouth

soft-bellied, wide-hipped, whole
lotta somethin'

banjo-pick tongue
pluck-pick-pluck-pick-pluck
love like brown chicken feathers

lard cornbread and moon water
the winter soup of your hands

a greened penny with a hole
through Abe's chest

black-cat footstep
oak-root steppin' stones

your bonfire-smoke-breaths
fill my living lungs
your voice, my voice
we whisper desperate prayers
as close to the skin as possible
as close to the flame as possible

Buried on our Bellies *by Dominque Feloss*

There is a screaming woman who lives in the field next to our house. I never see her when the sun is up, and she sounds more like she's wailing prayers to the moon. She's in despair most of the time. However, there are moments when her cries are filled with joy. Her tight, coily hair, a mix of black and grey, bounces as she jumps. She's conversing with the sky during those delicate moments, singing amongst the croaking frogs in her white dress. She's an odd woman who no one can see but me. I tried telling my mother and father, but no one believes me.

The woman turns to look at me in the quiet of the night. I'm so far away, peeping from my bedroom window. I'm shocked that she's noticed me, and I say hello. She holds her crooked finger to her mouth. Then she speaks to me as if I were only a foot away. The woman says to shush because the cicadas are speaking.

So, I listen.

They are loud like a symphony, and at first, I can't hear anything but their summer song. Then, slowly, it transforms into a hymnal, a bluegrass melody surrounded by holy incantations. Then, in plain words, the dictation becomes clear.

Come to the graveyard.

The woman's lips are mouthing the lyrics of the cicadas' song as she stares at me with her wild hair and wild eyes.

Come to the graveyard.

I don't know why I follow her. Perhaps something in my bones tells me to trust her. Nonetheless, I put my slippers on and throw a thin robe over my pajamas. I crack my bedroom window slightly and then throw it open quickly. Sounds are louder if you let them linger. I climb from the window and land on the soft grass with a slight thump. I've never gone out at night. But I have never heard the woman speak, nor have I heard the cicadas make demands. Tonight is a night full of nevers.

As I walk through the dark towards the field where the woman stands, I shiver. It is chilly for July, but nothing stops me from following the woman as she turns and dances to the graveyard by the church farther down the road.

The walk seems endless for a while. With each step I take, I succumb to the cold. I am freezing by the time I make it past the archway of the graveyard. My bones are rattling underneath my skin.

The woman's dance is slow now, somber. She's wailing sad prayers again, crying louder than the cicadas can sing. Her hair flows with the cold breeze as she continues to move towards the edge of the graveyard, where the trees sprout from the shadows. I am too far from the house, and now I am afraid. Why did I follow this woman to where bodies are buried beneath us?

She turns to me as her face disappears behind the tree line. Frightened, I slow my pace as I walk past the beautifully adorned graves, dates and dashes surrounded by roses and angels etched into the headstones. There is a child's grave where a weathered doll sits atop, its glossy eyes and smile hauntingly sad. And then, I too disappear behind the graveyard.

Trees loom over us like angry men. I cower underneath them, trying to stick to the sliver of moonlight that exists between their jagged branches. Ahead, the woman sulks and sways solemnly like she's on her way to the guillotine, exaggerated movements ghost-like under the cover of night.

And then, she stops.

She stands before a large rock covered in moss and grime. She points to it, beckons me closer. I follow. The closer I get, the colder I am. I couldn't see her eyes from afar, but now that I'm close, there is a film of milk painted over her eyes like she is dead. Her cheeks are sunken, and her mouth is open but stiff, like it's been frozen that way for a long while. And then, like magic, her open mouth says, *Dig.*

I am on my hands and knees now. My body is no longer obeying my commands, but rather hers, as my fingers begin scratching at the surface of the soil. My nails bend away from their beds as dirt fills the pockets of flesh. And then, I'm digging faster than humanly possible. And I finally touch something else made from the earth.

A skull.

Bodily autonomy reappears as I screech and jump away, falling over onto my back and covering my robe with loose soil. I brush myself off and get up. But I scream again, as I see there is now more than her and me in the forest. Now there are men, women, children, all dressed in simple white clothing. Their skin is different shades of brown and black, their hair full like clouds. Their eyes are full of milk and tears, too, and they dance. Their slow movements are a ritual of sorrow. Their mouths are not moving, but their dance tells a story.

We watched the church from underneath, the word of God construed.

The children begin to wail. Then the women, then the men. It seems to vibrate the trees that now feel sad instead of angry.

Then thrown into the ground and buried on our bellies.

I'm crying. I *see* their pain. I scratch at my eyes as I am forced to watch pastors give sermons through the cracks of a floorboard. These sermons tell us that we are cursed. Mistakes. They tell the people on top with their fans and their fancy wear that we are meant to obey. God says that it is okay to use our hair to stuff their chairs. It is okay to use our children as alligator bait. It is okay to have a feast under our swaying brothers. And when the liars die, they rot in white caskets with flowers and crowns while they throw us in pits on our bellies. It is our hands that place the stones, turn the dead towards the sky, until our hands tire, and we too, die.

My vision clears, and through my tears, I see the ghosts are now dancing joyously, through tears of their own.

But through death we are free, and this is our land now. The liars curse at us through the burning floorboards of hell, and we dance atop the flames.

Now, I am back in my bed. I cannot sleep. I cannot stop thinking of the woman who led me to her grave. I think about what she wants me to do. Maybe she wants me to burn down that house of evil and release their souls. Maybe my ancestors want to dance somewhere else. Maybe they are tired of being hidden behind a holy house that preached lies to their children.

And that was the last day I ever saw her.

West of Illinois *by Ash Lange*

20 white pills I hold in my hand
sweat dissolves them part liquid, making
pools in the cracks my grandpa
calls life lines. He was taught by a palm
reader when he was 16 years
old on the road somewhere west
of Illinois, building houses, about
to make a mother out of my grandma.

When I was 10 he read my palm and
said I would live to be 96 and would
marry a man who loved my laugh.
I never believed him—about either—
and in this moment
I think of his green eyes watering,
what thorn weeds grew among flowers.
I imagine swallowing again and again.

Grandpa, I love you, but I have had a nine-year-long
feeling something bad is about to happen.
Somewhere between a dash and a period,
my mother calls 3 times in a row,
and I answer to her shaking voice.
I ask if she's okay and she says she just had this strange
feeling something bad was about to happen.
And I put the plastic back in the drawer,
look at the line in the middle of my palm headed
west of Illinois, and imagine my 96th birthday.

Sorry, I'm Trying to Quit *by Clinton W. Waters*

Most of my memories
of you smell like smoke.
There's a way you held
each one just so,

the way you folded your
cricket legs one over
the other. Sometimes you
didn't smoke them at all,

just let them eat
themselves up from
tip to filter. You would watch them
as you ignored your own food.

Their labored breaths,
like yours, coated the
walls in that bruise-yellow
color I didn't notice

until the picture frames
were removed. Until everything you touched
was gone.

And even if my memories
could only shadow forth,
throw your shape against
the wall, I could still hold
the smoke. I could watch
it become silky gray strands
that drifted up and away
to oblivion. I could smell

the trail it left behind and follow it

back to that kitchen table with you.
No beer cans, no bier holding your body.

Just your head tilted to rest on your fist, your eyes so
heavy it hurt. 20 years later and that smoke was

my only magic trick. To conjure your shade and sit a
spell. The only way to draw closer to you.

But I have to stop. I
have a life I'm living now that I no longer wish
to cut short.

I hope you understand.

Wintergreen Lifesaver *by Emma Bryan*

You should learn how to drive a stick
He said with his hand on the gear shift
and his blue eyes burning into me.
His gaze felt cool, like a wintergreen mint
going down the throat.
My papaw. Not my blood, but he's mine.

We lay claim to things around here.
We take what we can get.

My daddy loves things that are free.
My momma calls him cheap, but I think
deep down, he's fighting the system in the ways he can.
Taking what he can get.

Where I'm from, we were taught to love, in theory.
We were taught to give, because you're supposed to.
We were taught to serve because that's the price you pay
for your entry to heaven.

We memorize the verses because the Bible said to,
because the pastor pounded the pulpit and beat it into us.

I never learned how to drive a stick, but my lungs
operate in manual transmission. "Remember to breathe,"
I say to myself through gritted teeth and clenched fists.

I swallow hard. A sharp coolness trails down, steadying
me. I remember how to breathe.

Found in the Country *by Bill McCann*

Along narrow roads
sit all manner and types of businesses:
Auctioneers
  (who sell what mom and dad accumulated, and farm
  machinery, too)
Bars and restaurants
  (usually in the same establishment)
Bed and breakfasts
  (to avoid hearing the in-laws snore)
Bowling alleys
  (that keep teens and trouble separated)
Car lots
  (where folks can get a car after theirs no longer runs)
Cemeteries
  (where grandma and grandpa now reside)
Churches
  (which give comfort to the living and bury the dead)
Farms
  (the business, or at least the hobby, of many)
Fire departments
  (run by volunteers to keep people and property safe)
Garages
  (help keep vehicles running as long as possible)
Gas stations
  (keep cars, trucks, and farm machinery running)
Junk yards
  (where cars and trucks go when they no longer run)
Salons
  (where a gal can get her roots touched up)
Schools
  (educating the next generation of farmers,
  maybe entrepreneurs)
Skating rinks
  (see "Bowling alleys," above)

Not seen at all in our community?
    A mall—and that's the truth, Y'all
life in the country is
    stretched out
        and perhaps inconvenient.
But few would trade country ways
    for nightly traffic jams
        on long (bypass) highways
        to get home to a tiny patch of green:
That is a rural dweller's nightmare.

She Taught Me to Slice Tomatoes
by Amy Le Ann Richardson

It starts with the right knife—
not sharp, but known,
its wooden handle worn soft
from decades of Julys.

She said, *"You don't rush a good tomato,"*
then taught me to let the blade glide,
not cut.

Let the fruit do the work.

We stood over the sink,
juice on our fingers,
sunlight catching the curve of her gold ring.

These were not just tomatoes.
They were stories
ripened on vines our people planted
before they had words for grief.

She told them like recipes:
A bit of sorrow, a heap of grit,
simmer it slow with laughter,
that's how you feed a family.

And I listened.

Not just to her words,
but to the way she turned them into music,
a kind of hymn you hum while canning beans,
or shelling peas in a summer lull
when the cicadas sing your grandmother's name.

Some folks think survival
is just making it through.
But we knew you had to sing while you stirred.
You had to dance barefoot in the kitchen
even when the water bill came pink.

This, too, is resistance:
passing down the way to pickle,
the way to mend a hem,
the way to hold a room with a story
until even sorrow listens.

I still use her knife.
Still hum while I slice.
Still plant too many tomatoes
just in case someone's hungry
for the kind of hope
you can taste.

I didn't know my brother when *by Lexie Stepro*

I called and told him that his mom might be dying.
His mom, who wrote him letters from the beach
and loved him hard, and mine.

We are bonded now by the way our mother reaches
out to hug us when the sedation agitates her/
the way the ventilator sings when she's about to choke/
through scenes I can't describe
to anyone else who loves me

and he's gentle in the way he silently sits with me
in the grass by the parking garage. Both of us
always thought there would be more time.
Neither of us are mechanics or miracle workers, but
"God works through the hearts and minds of men,"
he tells me. I spend most of the hours in the day begging
for a sign, while he just knows it's not over yet.
I want that type of peace to be made for me, too.
I need something to wash over me.

The first thing I do when I come back to Oldham County
is drive the backroads like I'm forgiving them.
I'm hoping they'll forgive me too.
I roll down all my windows and yell
thank you, thank you,
thank you.

It couldn't have all been so bad.
I'd do just about anything to go back.

Bloodroot and Belladonna *by Belle Townsend*

They say:
Be good,
like Sunday morning shoes
scuffed only on the inside.

They say:
Turn the other cheek,
as if our jawbones weren't already cracked
from turning too much.

Out here,
we gut deer clean
and keep our knives sharp.
We know what rot smells like
long before it hits the skin.

They want us holy,
barefoot and haloed in humility,
while they build mansions
from the bones of our neighbors,
and eat supper smiling
like nothing ever bled to feed them.

But here's the truth:
Mercy is a meal only the full can afford.
There's no heaven in submission.
No gospel in the gallows.

As for me and mine,
we plant bloodroot and belladonna.
We speak in shotgun gospel,
in rusted-out hymns
that rhyme with justice.

This is not hate. This is inheritance.
This is love with a blade.
So let them write their stories
where the many die noble and clean.
We'll write ours in fossil and fire.

We are the rifle
over the fireplace
finally taken down.

When the Clouds Don't Close *by NitaJade*

All night it rains and it rains and it rains and it rains and
the homeless remain homeless and it rains and the
backyard meth heads stay meth heads and it rains and
again my uncle's laid out on a park bench somewhere
and it rains (if anything it rains harder) it rains and
ushers in a dawn it rains and washes out a dusk it rains
and the stray cats don't have a box to cower under when
it thunders and it rains a night terror and it rains caged
mud onto tiny brown feet it rains a lake about the ankles
it rains an inverted umbrella it rains and some beast in
the distance announces its death or its birth it rains and
regurgitates storm drains it rains and crumples the tents
it rains bombs on babies it rains their blood on your
prayers it rains an oil-slick rainbow it rains a flash it
rains a flood onto my porch it rains a snake up to my
door it rains and reigns subconscious and rains when my
brother decides which version of himself to be it rains
the branch free of its tree it rains a street into a river, a
river into an ocean it rains when twice in two days she
condemns herself wicked it rains when the sun comes
out it rains still it rains stubborn when the devil beats his
wife it rains when the red don't rinse off quick enough it
rains and it rains REM cycles then it rains stock-still it
rains awake it rains a new day good God it rains!

When Grief Kisses Me *by Shiloh Stump*

I kiss back, with a tongue
hot like the underbelly
of my grandma's truck
teeth knocking on the door
of my mouth begging me
to open, open wider
to be a good little orphan
and swallow
memories thick and wet and heavy
to coat my throat in everything
I can't say to a body laying
rotten and earthed and impotent

Grief wants me to take him
doggy style, ride reverse cowboy
lying down flat on my back
reminds him too much of my mother
he says
there's enough time to lay flat
later, later
when the earth opens up
to swallow this body, later
for now I'll take him standing up
he likes it when I disobey

Grief's hand searches
in the drawer of my nightstand
for the condoms I bought
when I was feeling hopeful
and young and concerned
about what comes after,
the last time he stayed
the condom broke
oh shit, he said

looks like we've got to
trust each other now

I pull Grief's hand back to me
my face, my chest, my throat
he latches around me with fingers
tight like a casket
harder, I say
I feel his grip stiffen and I see stars
all the faces I thought
I'd someday forget
dance across my bedroom walls

Do you trust me
he asks
I pretend to forget all the other bodies
he'll taste and fill and enter
later, now
he's here
I don't trust he'll warn me
when he cums and screams
and wakes my neighbors
but I trust that this time, I'll scream
louder, make him beg
for seconds and pillow talk
and a well earned breakfast

He asks if he can stay the night
I lie and tell him I have to work early
and my sheets are dirty and there'll be
no time for seconds tonight
standing in the light of the doorway
his mouth half closed, half open
I tell him next time, I'll call him
and next time, it's my turn
to be on top.

Trashed *by Sullivan Potter*

There's an old, trashed recliner
just off the bank of some ridge top,
down on County Road 44.

Faded corduroy the color of bacon grease
stretches across brittle steel bones,
slouched in tree-dappled sunlight,
hardly conscious.

The mildewed arms are littered
with the wounds of extinguished cigarette butts,
scarring through bleached, threadbare fabric.

No ridgetop rainstorm or scorching sunbeam
can wash out the sweat stains
or lift the weight left in that seat cushion—
bruises embedded long before
it got tossed from some old truck bed.

That recliner's seen better days.
Ain't got no use no more.

There's a numbing comfort in being trashed.
In baking under a maple haze,
just out of view.

The rusted springs beneath the footrest
would prop themselves up for eternity
if they could.

Time blurs from dawn to dusk,
but that recliner still manages
to feel every throbbing second—
unaware of its skirted base

sinking deeper into leaf rot
and gripping mud.

God, I want to get trashed—
again and again—
so damn bad
I'm jealous of that recliner.

That roadside numbness…
you just can't beat that feeling.
God knows I've tried.

If You Fall In Love With A Cryptid *by Shaun Turner*

My hands are soft as moss on one side,
the other side is as sharp as bark on an old oak tree.
My voice will hum beneath your skin,
but you won't hear it in your dreams.

I'll crawl through the spaces in your lines,
become the rust on your old truck,
the sound of a computer rebooting
you'd thought you forgot. Love,
I'll be the shadow in the barn at dusk,
the hay bale in the field you forgot about.

You'll never catch me in a mirror,
just a glint of light among the treeline,
the taste of tobacco when you kiss me.

Instead of saying "I'd love you, like a confession,"
I will say, "I will let you learn the truth
in the way the rain speaks to the dust,
quiet and constant, until it sinks through."

Instead of saying "I'd pop you open
like a can of biscuits," please say,
"I will let you show yourself to me."
So slowly, I'll never even know who you are.

monologic *by Josh May*

and i hate you
        because you're different
               and that's all the reason i need
        because you're different
and i hate you

Biloxi Fever *by Trecinda Wilder*

It was Saturday night with a full moon, and, having walked through the damp weeds from the old shotgun house next door, Marcellus approached Mrs. Pollard and said to her, "I'z sorry, Mizzie Pollard, but he's passed out, a-lyin' in that ditch ag'in."

"Thank you for letting me know, Marcellus. Can you help me git him in the house please?"

"Yes'm."

Peeling paint fell for the hundredth time from the screen door that slammed as they trapsed together out toward the grassy ditch bank that ran alongside the well-worn country road. Under the full moon light, their 'mister' lay in a patch of grass that showed up three shades greener than the rest, on account of it sitting at the end of the soapy greywater runoff from the kitchen sink. They both eyed Mr. Pollard, his legs and arms invaded by stink bugs where his body met the ground. Mizzie grabbed his arms. Marcellus grabbed his legs. Peeling paint went flying again when the screen door slammed upon their return, cutting the thick Biloxi air as the mismatched couple maneuvered the dead weight of their sorry racist redneck patriarch toward the stained couch.

He lay on the worn couch until the early morning hours and threw up on the side. He fumbled through the moonlit parlor into the bedroom, knuckles white, hunting for his target, which he found in the dark warmth of her bed, and he rapped his fist against her face while his harrowed wife whimpered, knowing better than to cry. It would set him off again.

Another Saturday night came two weeks later, with a new moon and jet-black heavens except for the brilliant stars and river of the Milky Way that streamed above the house. "I'z sorry, Mizzie Pollard, but he's in that thar ditch ag'in."

Expelling a sigh that emptied her weak lungs, she eyed Marcellus, and he met her gaze, watching her shoulders slump even further as the corners of her mouth drooped almost past her chin line. Their mutual fatigue stitched up a heavy drop of time into a bag of bloody "what-if's" that they both acknowledged without words, and then they moved from the kitchen, being careful not to let that screen door slam this time.

Above their concerned heads, a bare bulb illuminated the haint blue ceiling of the porch. They looked both ways and moved toward that ditch bank again. She grabbed his arms. He grabbed his legs, and they maneuvered the embodiment of a violent patriarchal past toward the center of the warm asphalt. With the future hanging in the balance of the moment, they paused and listened together and heard a crow, some big ass gator grunting, and a truck in the distance.

"Care for some lemonade, Marcellus?"

Family History *by Elizabeth Roach-Smith*

Stealthily, she forges her concoction.
Mushroom clouds of steam envelop her as she works,
Cayenne peppering its aroma
Beyond the confines of the kitchen.
The ways of the grandmothers inspire her,
Aspics, stewed tomatoes and all
She nods to them by studying the family classics.
But finding they lack the spice she craves,
She folds her personality in
Along with the jalapenos.

She explores her culinary genealogy
Through baking, steaming, and frying,
The hiss of the oil in the cast iron pan
The luscious lard folded into the biscuit dough,
The blanched broccoli as emerald
As her great-aunt's wedding ring.

She is a sharp branch curled away from
The domesticity of her lineage,
The women who spent their days
Ironing, folding, scrubbing,
The original slow cookers
with no alternative.

She knows cooking as her vocation,
Sharpening her knives a daily sacrament,
Scrubbing carrots as tenderly as she would a child,
Slicing onions with the certainty of a guillotine.

Her strength and creativity
Shimmer like the tiny ruby studs she wears each day,
Her rich risotto and flaky Dover sole
Earning her plaudits and stars,

From restaurant critics and patrons
Who savor each fragrant course,
Straining to see the chef
Whose shoulders hunch ever higher
As the hour grows late.

At the end of service,
She kisses her fingertips,
Touching the amethyst pendant at her throat,
Passed down by the women before her.
Her recipe recorded in the family book,
The legacy continues.

show me where you live on your hand
by andrea lianne grabowski

my veins a thousand tiny lakes and rivers,
air around my skin an even handful of saltless oceans.
my father was raised in the soft flesh below my thumb,
motor city suburbs on my palm. drive a line to colonized
wilderness where i took my first breath. white pines
planted in calluses, my blood on top of Odawa soil.
every knuckle, an abandoned homestead, a field of corn.
a cherry orchard, star thistle, false legends of bears.
shipwrecks and plastic canoes, *this place is only meant
for spectators, snowbirds, ski-fiends,
faded flags and rifles.* but look—
the patch where i always pick wild blueberries,
rooted at the first bend of my pinkie.
every cell in my epidermis, a beach where waves
gusted me up and down and made me laugh with glee.
here is my lifeline, tracing the road up my skin
so it tickles. each branch a prophecy denied—
my roots will not grow in this sand,
the cornish pasties and apple cider will push me to
skyscrapers. but i've seen double rainbows here.
there's a gas station in the middle of nowhere
with closeted kids behind the counter, and
a trans girl buying cigarettes is the best part of their day.
we all see each other, between the flags and the fences.
clearer even than in the cities, on empty highways.
i watch for the deer in the dark.
their eyes gleam warnings—*this land is not yours.*
i cup trillium blossoms in my hands,
but do not pick them.
their pistils ask—*how do you build a home?*

The Knowing *by Caitlin Valentine*

Quietly, a woman enters the bar, and
She slides onto the cool vinyl to settle.
A reflection stares back into my eyes.

Hills embellished with emerald trees
Dance with scarves of mist against grey heavens
To greet each other like old friends.

An order is placed, medicine is measured.
We perform the ancient exchange.
Palpable is the shared pain between us.

The newcomer explains, I explain back.
Though stranger in this building,
The building far stranger to this land.

We enlighten each other, yammerin' in a language
Only kin would appreciate.
Discussing fissures and wounds
Only kin would understand.

Every word is filled with honeysuckle.
Our grannies and mamaws would smile
If they could also be here to sip a well shot.

But my granny is at work.
Disability checks are plenty but few.
And her mamaw passed a while back.
Will we retire in the same way?

Polite hands begin to move with tender purpose,
Assembling an organized discard pile,
Our green veins snaking through clutter to make haste.
Dividing the workload is natural.

Should we start a bluegrass band?
What if we opened up a diner and paid our bills on time?
We confess we've long been entranced by fae folk,
From the creek where ex Baptist women go to find god.
If luck shone down and we
lived our ancestors' wildest dreams,
Would we feel allowed to be content?

Bushwhacking *by Marjorie Maddox*

Bushwhack, he says, is not Ohioan (though
it plumes when I twang it, stretches
back, snaps, catapults each stick in the Adirondacks).
    Look
it up, my father says, voice tugging telephone lines.
An attacker. The War.
He the adventurer. The Scout. Sucking snake bites.
Cocking the gun, pelting everything in sight.
(Once we ate squirrel from the backyard. Suburbia.)

I've been saying it for days,
its tail wiggling in my throat, not-quite dead, dying.
There: stepping with too-heavy of a pack
up stone, rotted trunks, wet moss—
all stacked up to make a mountain. (My foot slips.)
    Ahead,
someone says it. Bushwhack.
Behind, it bites my ankles like a black fly,
whacks me on the ass till I smile and,
surprised, like who I am.
My hips ache. I tighten
my straps, side-step a mud-creek,
teeter on stones the shape of
muffins I'm munching. Bushwhack, he mutters,
flipping pages as I heave up: flat rock at the top,
Mohawk valley dropped and splattered all over (we are
both right. Or close) so that, now, again,
some branch tattooing itself on my shoulder,
I could high-jump, pogo-stick it to the edge,
high enough and wide.

Charred Tobacco *by Zachary Poehlein*

He marked his progress with burnt and spent cigarette butts. Some still had a thimble full of charred tobacco that spilled out when returning to pages where he'd left off. There were smudges and stains left on the lily sheaves, and it was nice to think of them as little parts of his mind, sloughed off and abandoned, marking where he had retired. He couldn't read the words on the page, he just liked the way some of 'em looked, laid out in neat rows and even lines. So he anointed each furrow of letters with ash and soot, stale smoke and singed margin. He added his mark to shapes and forms he couldn't understand. He found other ways to contract meaning from the thin leaves. He lingered among passages concerning angels and demons. Wheels of light in the sky. Burning apparitions of God's Love or God's Wrath.

Allen's Country Store: Corinth *by Bill McCann*

I

Mayonnaise
Pickles
Pliers
Tires
The Grant County News
    (And *the Cynthiana Democrat,* too?)
Hunt Brothers Pizza
Hunting licenses
Videos
Romance novels
Fishing line
Kite string
Peanut butter
Spackle
Fishing tackle
Flashlights
Gas
Bread
Thread
Nuts and
Bolts of fabric?
            Nope, there were limits

II

Fire came and,
like every efficient maid,
left nothing but a bit of ash
in what used to be the basement
but is now the only floor
of a place
            that is no more.

III

The basement is once again a basement.
An I-beam is set and cross beams
       hold up a new floor.
Walls are going up.
Soon there will be a new "Allen's"
Lacking fire or catastrophe,
       the new building will last as long as the first.
Alas, the new store may not survive.
For while owners and county planners dithered,
Dollar General built a new space to sell Corinthians
       Cheaper mayonnaise and,
       perhaps,
           even nuts,
       and bolts of fabric.

Norma *by Rachel Rosolina*

There exists a pure moment in childhood,
small still, sheltered by matriarchs tender,
when the world's filament glows gold with good,
when sweet sun-warmed tea radiates splendor.
Rising biscuits, jam tops popping, her hand
brushing hair from my face as she laughs, laughs.
Tales from her own youth, hooky and headstands.
Glinting remembrance hiding just enough.
Mornings spent prospecting yard sale treasures—
idolized lamps or glass grapes or faux gems
blaze brightly as summer's gleaming pleasure.
The day's burnished shine forestalls evening's dim.
    Stirred to unfetter, she softly discerns
    three stacks of memories: keep, sell, and burn.

One Foot on Each Bank of the Creek
by Susanna Spearman

[Lavelle, my mother's mother's mother]

mountain girl child
born in Lothair Perr
a place with a beautiful name
certainly a place that is dark dark green

in this place
the mountains are close together
folks in the holler are close together
her seven children are close together
and bound up with all her pain
and whatever love she can muster
whatever love is left after her husband hits her
whatever love is left after she feeds them all
whatever love is left after she says
it is
what it is
what it is

[Betty, my mother's mother]

mountain girl child
born near Pond Creek
she could hear its water rushing
as she raised her six siblings in that place
beautiful and dark and dark green

sometimes
the mountains felt too close together
sometimes her father's fists felt too close
together with the bodies of his children
she left for nursing school so she could learn

to heal what hurts
she left as much as she could of her accent behind
her pastor called her a *Hillwilliam*
tamed out enough of her Appalachian wild
tamed enough of her pain
to be content
it is what it is
but it isn't enough

[Kathryn, my mother]

mountain girl child
grown green away from the
holy peaks and dark valleys
her songs were sung across
the burials of Michigan snow drifts
or the humid baptism
of Atlanta summers

she wonders aloud sometimes
why no one talks to their neighbors
anymore
where it is she might find
her people
it isn't enough

[Susanna]

mountain girl child
of the ones who left
and stayed away
my blood is
get out so you can be somethin'!
I'm made of hunger
for a place
I do not really know

but I tell ya
there was never enough
on the new land
those Carolina foothills
never enough echo
never enough
the dark not dark enough for starlight
the green not green enough for family

Booking *by Cassandra Ruby*

Blue-suited muthafuckers spitting in our faces with
ideologies of what species we ought to be.
Chicano. Tattooed.
We fit the description.
I stand there,
maintaining my right
to remain silent.
Waiting on the buzz for entrance.
Two hands,
un-cuffed,
casually placed on the wall.
Prepared for the pat-down.
Sliding the coarse orange shirt over my head.
Watching my man,
in his cage,
mouthing *I love you.*
Home.
Assimilating to their ideologies.
Species: Chicano/Gangster/Criminal.

Memento Mori *by Charlie/Boo Mariano Reynolds*

Visions of death populate my home town
Looming constantly on the periphery.
Anonymous rotting wooden crosses round the curve
Standing over the possums and raccoons on the road.
In the fall it's deer strung up on racks to drain.
In the spring we wake and in the barn it's
Newborn piglets crushed under their mama,
Lives quashed before they'd hardly begun, and
A sign by the driveway: "Rabbits: for food or as pets."
The headless chicken. Something dies and something
lives.

News of death populates my home town,
Spoken solemnly as rumour or simple fact.
Junior took a bullet during the hunting trip;
Sally flew down the dirt road hill too fast;
Uncle fell off the fishing boat and into the motor;
Mr. Keenan fell putting a new roof on the old barn;
Did you hear about the barfight last summer?
We're taking Spot's kid to the slaughterhouse;
We had to take Fido out behind the barn;
The horse kicked, then when the bull got loose

I knew that I too will die someday and become this
          week's news,
That my gravestone will go in the old cemetery by the
          library
Where cars drive by without a glance where the bugs
          will feast on me
Like a car-wrecked dirt-road raccoon and I knew that I
          will die.

Kept / Not Kept *by Jan Wiezorek*

Kept /

Grandmother Nana's ruby red glass bell
Rock from Cherry Beach, dated 7.1.69
Old flour sack from Niagara Mills
Eleven, of First Holy Communion, May 1962
Vial of "Real Gold," panned at Knott's Berry Farm, 1964
Grandmother Nana's memorial prayer card, 2001
Me, protesting at Washington Park, 1968, singing "We Shall
Overcome"
Walking in the woods at the state park, Altar Boys' Picnic,
May 1968
Singing before the State Senate, Spring 1972
Singing with "my band" in uncle Mick's basement, 1967
My first bar drink, strawberry Hopalong Cassidy sarsaparilla,
age 5, 1960
Bowling for the first time, score 50, one strike, fourth grade
Dad's new car, black Chevy, 1959
Eating sno-cones, with colored "blue" lips, county fair

Not Kept /

Brother lying on the beach, Honolulu, 1959
Four stacked wooden dolls, painted, Japanese, 1960
Bottle cap opener in the shape of a guitar
Set of spoons from Wall Drug, 1973
Dodge Dart, four doors, olive green, automatic transmission,
1972
Four portraits of kittens, strays
Farrah Fawcett poster
Portable radio, ball and chain design, Christmas, 1976
Polaroid Swinger camera
Clip-on ties, two or three
Polyester leisure suit
Sting-ray bicycle with banana seat
Bottle cap opener, flowered, Austin, Minn., 1975
Eating, Tom Thumb donuts, one dozen, county fair

The Teachings of Jesus Christ *by Ash Lange*
after working on a farm in the country, 2023

Today, there is no work, so I cry to get it out—because I
miss talking about what I like to talk about
and kissing someone on the mouth.
Last night she let down her hair for the second time,
but this time we were alone. I store the secret in the heart
of my stomach and remember the first time I saw it
like this when we were both 11 years old.

Out here, so many confessions are left untold.
The Teachings of Jesus Christ—
she's washing it in her kitchen sink
with soap she made, and
I'm trying again and again to look away.
Jesus said something about the lust of the flesh.

The water from the wash flows into the white plastic
bucket under the sink.
I want to be the bucket so bad I start to cry.
The Teachings of Jesus Christ—
I look anywhere but her green eyes and wish
that in another life
I was her husband
and she
was my wife.

idyll, broken *by andrea lianne grabowski*

i.
red wagon of dolls on saffron road,
i dragged rusting wheels up gravel dust.
our painted mailbox already rusted.
bleeding hearts drooped from their stems.

ii.
wild blueberry patch sour and small,
between the white pines. my life itself,
sour and small, tangy with lonesome
imagination, harvesting blueberry bucketfuls
from cultivated fields across deadstream road.

iii.
wading in the cold creek, very much alive, i had
no forewarning, no fears. this stream
would die someday, perhaps. like the tree
whose roots were ripped from stable soil,
somewhere. losing its pebbles to my small,
grasping hands. like sweetness of this life, lost to—

iv.
one white pine, i called the school tree.
a lone pine, like the party store by the drive-in.
always observation, never experience. the
school tree wasn't enough. lost to some
educational search, mountains, broken
speed limits. my lonesome imagination
tightened itself around my chest. protection.

v.
no forewarning. cedar trees silent to my
unmoored self. like the mountains would be.
like god would be. like desire would be.

some fears. white truck of dolls leaving
saffron road, turquoise bicycle sour with
the memory of rainbow silk. the oak tree
would shrink, otter creek would reach,
lake michigan waves would curl over my feet,
pulling, begging, keeping.

Come and Take It *by Brandon Sun Eagle Jent*

Barren soil be damned, I've planted peace
seeds in my garden and I refuse to uproot.
No, I know I'll see peace blossom
in the spring, lush green bouquets
laid on every doorstep my hands can
reach, each wrapped in pink ribbon,
my favorite color. Since birth I've worn
the maw of the American monster—
fangs for a necklace, corpse breath
cologne. I'll roll peace into blunts
and strike matches on its hard palate,
hotbox the beast's roaring corridor.
Should this bear trap catch, let it choke
on my entrails. Bile won't rid my lips
of the smile that stains them.

Reverberations *by Andre Zoolalian*

The dulcimers resound,
and the room reflects time.

The frequencies meet the history,
this house, a testament
to then and now.

The walls hold the colors, hues of time.
The floors once knew the rhythm
of jovial Shaker stomps.

And the room which held sweet songs and claps
is reverberated by time.

Or, another time,
the oil stains, blotting the floor
like industrial raindrops
of a gilded generation,
as the mechanic worked with the art of chrome
and the medicine of rock 'n' roll.

As the dulcimer band concludes,
I wonder how this room
holds everything at once.

The Cottonwoods scatter a summer snow
by Arielle Theobald

floating fluff balls swimming
through the forests and towns,
tickling your cheeks and nose,
like dandelion seeds raining
from the tops of trees.

Summer in the Sun Valley between
mountains means less and less
specifically, more and more like
a memory. If I have children,
will they still dream of the glory season?
Or just reprieve from educational litany.

Summer in Hailey, Idaho
was once perfectly drearily
white hot. Every jeweled day
held the potential dare of jumping
in the freezing, snow-run-off river;
every night could be spent sleeping
on the trampoline in the backyard
and counting shooting stars.

Perhaps the seasons have simply pushed
forward, giving us temperate Septembers.
Or perhaps everything, by natural law
is changing. Am I of the last generation
to have known, to remember
the fresh breath of spring
and the warm lust of her follower?

And what of the trees,
will they keep snowing
in the middle of summer?

Redbuds *by MJ Hatfield*

I decided to still love you in the springtime.
Last year, the two of us in a car,
hugged tight between green-blue hills
with purple dotted here and there, on a trip down home.

I warned you how long a drive it would be, to
not get the water in your eyes when you washed
your hands, and that we had to stop and get snacks
at my favorite gas station on the way.
You wanted to try everything I bought.

Your hand pressed firm against the glass
like my Chevy was a tour bus.
"What is that tree everywhere?"
"Them's redbuds."
No one ever asked me about a Judas tree like that,
something that was everywhere, so beautiful, but so sad.
Dripping blood forever and ever.

I decided to still love you
even though I will bleed and bleed
at least once a year. Cursed to keep atoning
for my sins.

You'd hold me tight no matter if I was grey or green or
blood red-purple.

You accept all of me, even though the water will burn
your eyes.

Encounters With the Sweet By and By
by Marianne Peel

I left fragments of stories
under the rungs of the bar stools.
Spooled out tales
while nursing an Old Fashioned
and never told you how I was
on a Delta flight in an aisle seat
when my father died. My brother
shaved him with a straight razor.
Pressed ice chips between his teeth.
And my brother told me to write the eulogy
the night before a collage of strangers
tethered to walkers and canes and oxygen tanks
gathered at the restaurant because they heard
the guacamole was fresh, prepared tableside
by a chef with no thumbs. They had come
for the carnival act, wanting to see
how he held the knife to the flesh
of the avocado. A curiosity shoppe
of mourners.

I remember looking out the Allegheny Air
plane window as a child. In my periphery,
a full-grown man stands in the aisle
and touches both windows with his wing span.
Swishing sounds emerge from his mouth
as he navigates wind currents. I found
the face of a god in the space above the clouds.
Not Jesus on a tortilla. Not the Virgin Mary
on a sausage and gravy biscuit. I spied a woman
with nose piercings, ear piercings, belly button
piercings. Lavender lipstick. Gold shimmer shadow
on her eyelids.

She plays a reedless oboe. Masterful at circular
breathing. I offer castanets for her fingers,
a tambourine for a crown.

The saints in my growing-up house were bloodied.
A crown of barbs, thorns piercing forehead flesh,
piercing naked soles, piercing surfaces of scalps.
No admittance to Mass without the bobby pins
gouging the scalp, holding the doily in place.
Paintings bled onto the wood planks
in the hallway. Worried their way into tongue
and groove. That space where my knees served their
penance. A prerequisite to the waiting room of
purgatory. We moaned prayers for the poor souls in
purgatory every night. My mother's funeral cards,
catalogued by death date. A litany of souls
beseeched out of limbo.

On the night I was married, my new husband drove me
to the cemetery. Introduced me to his relatives under the
weeds. Ice on the gravestones in March. The ivy still a
pale green, wrapped around the tombstones
like a relentless spring, like determined kudzu.
And he pointed to the dashes on each stone.
Stones waiting for the chisel of the caretaker.
Guests who had just contorted their bodies into the
Chicken Dance or the fox trot would be here,
under our boot soles, underfoot, someday.

My daughter danced in the headlights of her car
the night her boyfriend's arm was severed
on a highway overpass. Bridge freezes before
the road surface.

Cautionary yellow signposts.
All those cubicles of ashes, like post office boxes,

each with its own skeleton key.

And my daughter danced herself into his ashes.
Her radio dialed up. Car doors open to the cemetery air.
The way she danced, on point,
the arch of her feet leaving behind
the soundless footprints
of a ballerina.

Promised Wrath *by Zachary Poehlein*

Peering over the horizon, I see rain in the west.
Tornadic cells of evil chilled breath
building infinite temples of spontaneous destruction.
Spinning whirls of fists hang like guillotines,
a promised wrath.
When the storm does reach our ridge,
there is an unbelievable fracturing of electric
night sky,
such that when I step out underneath the oak to piss,
the whole of heaven shatters,
and reveals itself,
before stitching back together
in triumphant clapping.
Some rumble,
some shudder of the curtain that is rain,
and dusk,
and impenetrable dark, tearing.
We speak of only roundness.
Only of circle never broken.
Struggling against the friction of each storm front,
I hush.

Go On: The Cicada Poem
by Willie Edward Taylor Carver Jr.

Written in a brief window of freedom.

There are over one trillion cicadas in Kentucky at the
moment.

As we drive they are splattering against the windshield.
Solid hits like bullets. And I am here watching it
happen, and I just wanna roll down the window and
scream at them. To tell them
to fly harder,
            to climb,
                  to fuck in broad daylight,
                        to sing until the stars hear them.

I know what it's like to be buried for 17 years.
I know what it's like to feel the color shorten in the
            remaining days.
I know what it's like to hear people complain about your
            noise.

I want to hand them all bottles of water and lit cigarettes
and say,

"Go on with it, bub. Life's calling. Get it."

what we keep *by Samantha Ratcliffe*

everything emaciated—
horse ribs and lungs that can't
push past getting there
snouts search muddy grass
just like we shovel past
empty dvd boxes
space heaters
a hundred dirty forks
blame the cat for most of that
bottles and bottles of pain
pills with no refills, still no
body is healing.

a cat named Nosey tries
to say goodbye the only way
she knows how
leaning her weight
against your loss.

and you
your tiny hands
so full of lighters,
though you have nothing left to light.
right there's my best friend
you say about a heated blanket.
when the women we know die
we dig them up.
out of the thrifted stored trinkets
swaddled and tired in their belonging
like it's in their blood to burrow
to fold away finely
into possession
into the weight of being
possessed.

Afterword: For Those Who Listened
by Belle Townsend

Thank you for reading this, for carrying these voices a little farther. If *Discarded* was an emergence, then *Testament* is what follows: the steady hum that reminds us we're still here, still building something together.

This anthology was never meant to be a map of what's broken, but a record of what endures: care, memory, courage, and the refusal to let anyone else tell us who we are. In a world that profits from our division, choosing to understand one another, to listen across distance and difference, is its own kind of rebellion.

The truth is that we have more in common than we've been told. Our neighbors are not our enemies; they're the ones who keep the porch light on when everything else goes dark. The real power sits above us, shaping stories to keep us apart. But what's made by hand, in community, always finds its way back to the surface.

Thank you for being part of that return. For reading, sharing, and holding what's here with care. This work, like the land and like us, grows through connection.

Please take time to read the bios included below of the contributors whose offerings make up the book in your hands. Reach out. Connect with them.

Y'all take care now!

With gratitude and hope,
Backwoods Literary Press
backwoodsliterarypress.com

Surabhi Balachander grew up in Indiana and is an assistant professor in the School of Writing, Literature, and Film at Oregon State University in Corvallis. Her book-in-progress seeks to define rural identity in American literature from 1920-2020, the U.S.'s first century as a majority-urban nation, and shows that rural America, in contrast to popular stereotypes, is best understood as multiethnic and cosmopolitan. Her work appears in *ISLE: Interdisciplinary Studies in Literature and Environment* and *Western American Literature.*

Makayla Danielle Gay hails from Southeastern Kentucky. Her debut poetry collection, *Hackles*, is out now.

Clinton W. Waters was born and raised in Bowling Green, Kentucky, where they received a BA in Creative Writing from WKU. Their work has been featured in *Still: The Journal* and *Untelling Magazine.*

Noah Edgar is a writer whose origins can be traced back to Cleveland, OH, though he is currently residing in Lexington, KY as an undergraduate student at the University of Kentucky.

Idris Isaiah Irihamye is a Rwandan-Kentuckian currently based in the Bluegrass with big holler dreams! They are a poet, agroecologist, and abolitionist currently engaged in youth environmental justice work and deepening their multi-media artistic practice. There is a

90% chance that Idris is preparing a cup of tea at this very moment.

Beth Feagan (she/her) grew up in southcentral Virginia, the Piedmont region. Midway between the mountains and the ocean, tobacco country, poor. She has lived all over but went back home to raise her son so he could grow up in her childhood woods and swimming hole. Since 2013, she has taught at Berea College in Kentucky, where she has put down new roots, but she still goes home for holidays and backyard stew.

Em Shepardson is a queer creative, care worker, and organizer raised by and returned to the driftless region of Southeast Minnesota.

Amanda Jo Slone is a writer, mother, and educator from Pike County, Kentucky. Her work is inspired by the pull of memory and the landscape she calls home.

Zachary Poehlein (he/him) is a proud Kentuckian, writer, and co-creator of Derby City Midnight. Born riverside, he can be found perched atop a hill in Central Kentucky.

Willie Edward Taylor Carver Jr. is an LGBTQ+ youth advocate and KY Teacher of the Year. His *Gay Poems for Red States* (University Press of Kentucky) is a World Pride, Stonewall, Whippoorwill, ALA, Read Appalachia, and Book Riot award recipient. His novel, *Tore All to Pieces*, arrives 2026 (University Press of Kentucky). Willie writes from Appalachia and believes everyone's story matters.

Andre Zoolalian was born in Louisiana and is studying audio production and creative writing. He has a burgeoning dedication to poetic writings in particular, with his poetry recently being featured in the *Asbury Review* and *Armenian Weekly*. As a music producer, his primary genres are hip hop and R&B, with his production being recognized by the Universal Hip Hop Museum in the Bronx. With Southern roots and Irish and Armenian ancestry, he strives to bring a unique voice whether he's highlighting past and present collective injustices, sentimental absurdism, or nature.

Thailan Franklin is a Black, queer writer and academic from Bowling Green, Kentucky. They currently reside in Louisville, where they work as an Admissions Counselor at the University of Louisville. Thailan's writing is rooted in themes of love, loss, and existential embodiment and is shaped by their experience being raised by Black women from rural Kentucky.

Susanna Spearman (they/she) is a queer, Appalachian poet originally from South Carolina. They have an MFA in Creative Writing from Bluegrass Writers Studio. They live in central Kentucky with their wife, four cats, and a senior chihuahua. They are the secretary of Kentucky State Poetry Society and one of the editors of the KSPS semi-annual literary journal, *Pegasus.* They are the director of Multifarious Collective, an organization based in central Kentucky that amplifies multilingual/multicultural poetic and artistic voices.

andrea lianne grabowski is a midwestern dyke and 21st-century spinster occupying Anishinaabe land in so-called michigan. her writing lives in many indie lit homes and the self-published chapbook, *there is an earth after innocence.* you can find her on long drives, inspired by music, making zines, or lost in the woods.

Sullivan Potter is an Appalachian artist, storyteller, and poet from the foothills of southeast Ohio. His work blends visual art with writing and prose, celebrating the familiar while challenging stereotypes in Appalachian narratives. A current BFA student at Ohio University, Sullivan affectionately describes himself as 'just another redneck, taken by the American dream.'

Charlotte Isenberg (she/her) is a Western North Carolina Native whose writing explores the cultures and peoples of the Carolina foothills. As a Cherokee writer, her work focuses on themes like Indigenous sovereignty, reproductive justice, and the ways Appalachian and Indigenous cultures intersect towards those visions.

Ellen Pauley Goff (she/her) was born and raised in Kentucky, and her work always returns to her family's roots in the rural pockets of Appalachia, from Cumberland County to the hills of West Virginia. Her published short fiction and poetry can be found in the *Indiana Review, New Millennium Writings*, and the *Atlanta Review*, among others. Her debut novel, The Farewitch of Foxe Holler, is set in Kentucky and is forthcoming from Saga Press/Simon & Schuster on July 7, 2026.

Angel Ballew is a Georgia native and longtime Eastern Kentucky resident, a farmer, educator, and business operations specialist dedicated to purposeful food production and community building. She combines her love for the land with her expertise in business to nourish her community through farming, art, and collaboration. Through her partnership with Mountain Association, she also provides entrepreneurial coaching and business support to farmers and ag-based businesses.

Rook Bell is a queer, trans poet born and raised in Lawrenceburg, KY, currently attending college in Morehead, KY. Xyr works are an exploration of grief, hope, and the generational cycles we are all trying to outrun, all underscored by a stubborn and questionably requited love for the world, despite it all.

NitaJade is an Affrilachian Poet from Asheville, NC. They insist that their late O.G. Queen's sweet potato pie epitomizes love, and they aspire to embody the aesthetics of sloths and narwhals (slarwhals, if you please). They laugh loudly and stubbornly.

Anna Hurd is a queer archivist and writer from Adams County, Pennsylvania, currently living in Burlington, Vermont. They received their BA in English from the University of Vermont, their MS in Library and Information Science/Archives Management from Simmons University, and their inclination to poke around in creek beds and cemeteries from their dad's side of the family.

Shaun Turner is a writer, poet, and marketing specialist from Southeast Kentucky. His writing has been published in *The South Carolina Review, The Chattahoochee Review, Tin House Online,* and *the Appalachian Review*, where he was awarded the Denny C. Plattner Award in Fiction.

Born and raised in Carter County, Tennessee, **Rachel Rosolina** is Senior Director of Connection and Communication for Appalshop. A graduate of Berea College and West Virginia University, Rosolina has had work published in *Still: The Journal, Women Speak*

anthologies, Hellbender Magazine, and *Belt Magazine.*
She currently lives in Bloomington, Indiana, with her
husband and tiny cat.

Nefi Sanchez is a twenty-year-old poet from Southeast
Iowa who loves capturing the stories of people around
him. Since seventh grade, he has been leaving crumbs of
himself all over stolen notebooks, fast food receipts, and
foggy car windows in the form of poetry. He is currently
drifting through life, figuring out his future and its many
paths, all the while trying to hold onto as much of the
present as possible.

Ariadne Alexis Macquarie (she/they), originally from
Western North Carolina, is an MFA student at the
University of Kentucky. She is the editor-in-chief of *New
Limestone Review* and *On Gaia Literary Magazine,* and
is a staff reader for *Sundress Publications.* Her work can
be found in *Red Branch Review, YNST Magazine,
Women of Appalachia,* and elsewhere.

Samantha Ratcliffe is a second-year poetry MFA
candidate and graduate assistant at the University of
Kentucky. Originally from Pikeville, Kentucky, her
songwriting and poetry have been deeply influenced by
her roots. Her works have been published in *White Wall
Review, Untelling, Pegasus*, and elsewhere.

Bayley Hope Amburgey (she/they) is a Black, queer,
Appalachian artist and community organizer from
Eastern Kentucky who currently lives in Louisville, KY.
She uses her online platforms to organize mutual aid
campaigns and educate folks on local, national, and
international topics. Bayley is a writer, singer, and
currently works in education-based nonprofits.

Arielle Theobald (she/her) is a poet raised by the sea in Palos Verdes, California, who grew up spending summers in Hailey, Idaho, where her grandparents now live. Her work traces landscapes of queerness, belonging, and the natural world.

C.A. Osborne (he/him) is a working class poet with roots in Texas and Kentucky. He explores themes of Southern culture, poverty and addiction.

Pauletta Hansel was born and raised in southeastern Kentucky, with family roots in western North Carolina and southwest Virginia. Her recent books are *Will There Also Be Singing?* published by Shadelandhouse Modern Press and *Heartbreak Tree* published by Madville Publishing.

Shaelyn Bishop is an Assistant Professor of Biology, an artist, and a wishful writer from southcentral Kentucky. Her backgrounds in environmental studies, evolutionary biology, and sustainability inform both her work and creative pursuits.

Ash Lange (she/they) is a writer and food and climate justice advocate from Somerset, Kentucky, now living in Louisville's South End. Their work—both creative and technical—centers stories around climate change, the food system, rural and urban spaces, poverty, disability, and queer identity.

Shiloh Stump is a Two-Spirit (Kanien'kehá:ka and Tsalagi) mechanic, poet and full-time lover of all things bread related. When they're not investigating how the human heart is transformed by grief and kinship, they're wrenching on cars and coordinating events at The Pond in Letcher Co, KY with a gaggle of community members.

Belle Townsend is a queer writer, publisher, and organizer raised in rural western Kentucky. They are the Communications Director for the Kentucky State AFL-CIO, the statewide federation of 60+ labor unions. Belle is also the founder and editor in chief of Backwoods Literary Press, working at the intersection of labor, art, and community in Frankfort, KY. They received a BA in Political Science from Boston University in 2022. Their work includes a few chapbooks, and their writing has appeared here and there for this and that.

Cara Ellis (she/her) is an Appalachian organizer and activist. She previously served as the President of Pikeville Pride, an LGBTQ+ non-profit dedicated to strengthening visibility and inclusion of LGBTQ+ folks in Eastern Kentucky. With extensive experience in political campaigns as well as local and statewide policy work, Cara strives to work across ideological differences to find common ground and build strong interpersonal relationships in order to seek a shared vision for the future that benefits us all.

Originally from Avery County, North Carolina, **Audrey Nidiffer** is a First Year Writing instructor at Appalachian State University. She is strongly motivated by the belief that everyone has a story to tell. Audrey is proudly part of the mountains where she was raised which, like her, have been shaped by time and language.

Charlie/Boo Mariano Reynolds (he/they) is a queer, trans, and disabled writer/editor/musician/crafter/freak hailing from the farms and forests of Michigan.

Currently, he is stuck in the city for his education, where they have edited and had work published in *Swallow the Moon.*

Ellie Bee is a queer Tisay storyteller, community researcher, foodmaker, and barista from Jessamine County, Kentucky. Haunted by hordes of feminine ancestors denied their love as power, she uses evidence of restoration and resilience as clues to learn, document, and live their truth.

Melissa Helton is Literary Arts Director of Hindman Settlement School in Knott County, Kentucky. Her work has been in *Shenandoah, Women of Appalachia Project, Still: The Journal,* and more. Her chapbooks include *Inertia: A Study,* and *Hewn.* She is editor of the anthology *Troublesome Rising: A Thousand-Year Flood in Eastern Kentucky* and *Untelling,* the literary and arts magazine.

Brandon Sun Eagle Jent (he/she/they) resides in eastern Kentucky on the unceded lands of the ᎠᏂᏴᎤꮻ, S'atsoyaha, and Šaawanwaki nations. He writes poetry as an extension of a lifelong dialogue between herself, their kin (human and more-than-human), and the natural world.

Cola Day is a writer, student, and teacher from the West Virginia coalfields now based in New York City. Her writing is inspired by the many things that remind of home like loud rivers, Sundays in May, and love in hard places. Outside of writing, she loves hiking and doing sunrise yoga with her cat Maple.

Dominque Feloss is a philanthropic professional and writer originally from South Florida and is now based in Atlanta, Georgia. She is the 2024 John Lewis Writing Grant recipient for fiction and currently supports the Income, Wealth, and Arts portfolios at the Community Foundation for Greater Atlanta. Her background is in community impact work for both the public and nonprofit sectors, and she holds an MFA in Creative Writing from Maharishi International University.

Caitlin Valentine is a multimedia artist, specializing in performance arts and writing. She was raised in the Bluegrass by Eastern Kentucky folk and attended Northern Kentucky University. Now residing in Louisville, where she can usually be found dancing, modeling, gardening, and creating.

Brook West is a wordsmith, training developer, and founder of *Story Behavior*, a storytelling consulting resource that helps creatives engage the hidden logic of stories. The bones of Brook's ancestors have resided in central Kentucky longer than its stone fences, a gravity that draws her back whenever she tries to leave. Her work explores lessons related to belonging.

Elizabeth Roach-Smith grew up in the railroad town of Midway, Kentucky, where she spent her childhood creating fantastical stories, catching crawdads on her grandparents' farm, and reading books in a treehouse. She now lives in Louisville, Kentucky with her family and Great Pyrenees, working in communications while writing poetry and short stories.

Cassie Andresen (she/they) is a queer poet and musician from Southern Washington who currently lives in Seattle with her wife. She writes and performs art exploring feminism, queerness, sobriety, grief, and disability advocacy. Cassie can often be found playing guitar, crafting new non-alcoholic beverages, and finding a body of water to jump in.

Mark Alan Boykin is a writer, guitarist, programmer, organizer, and University of Chicago graduate who resides in Ashland, Kentucky. He performs as a singer/songwriter under the name Rogue Sheep.

christa kaodi is a poet and storyteller with Nigerian roots and an Appalachian upbringing. Her work reframes and adds context to our language, our culture, and our process of self-examination. As a translator between Kentucky and Nigerian cultures, christa kaodi writes poetry in what she knows of English, Igbo, and the language of Black love. Her work invites folks to reframe their understanding of belonging, love, and the origins of joy.

Jay McCoy is a poet and visual artist with deep Appalachian roots in Eastern Kentucky. He currently works with Kentucky Humanities as the Director for the Kentucky Book Festival and the Kentucky Center for the Book. Jay co-founded two active monthly reading series in Lexington, Kentucky, and co-hosts the weekly radio show, Kentucky Writers Roundtable, on RadioLex, 93.9 FM.

With roots in the Bluegrass, **Leigh Claire Schmidli** has also called Thailand & Holland home—but she always returns to Kentucky. She writes poetry, essays, & fiction, enjoys reading work with lyrical leanings, and cooks elaborate meals that remind her of the places she's called home. She'll use onions in just about anything, even a story.

MJ Hatfield is a Queer Appalachian who grew up in Clay County, KY. She currently lives, works, writes, and produces cabaret shows in Louisville. She loves The Wizard of Oz and her chihuahua, Cornbread. You can find her elsewhere at http://mjhatfield.carrd.com.

christiana cantrell (they/any) is a queer storyteller, poet, educator, and community tender from rural southeast Missouri. A lover of the oft-overlooked, christiana dedicates their time to feeding the people's minds, stomachs, and spirits through the work of their pen and their hands. They currently daydream in East Tennessee and can be found both out in the mountains and down in the streets.

Bill McCann, MFA, MA, MEd teaches at Eastern Kentucky University. He is a poet, playwright, and essayist. His memoir—*Yearnings: A Memoir in Prose and Poetry* (Cyberwit.net, 2025) is available now. His chapbook, *The New Adventures of Jesus* (Finishing Line Press, 2025) has also been adapted for the stage as a 10-minute play.

Trish J. Gibson is a photographer and writer from North East Tennessee, currently based in Lexington, Kentucky. Their works are built of familial archaeology, exploring the relationship between gender, violence, generational trauma, escape, and the Appalachian South.

Ell Havoc (she/her) is a political columnist, musician, and activist raised in the foothills of coal country, her work and commentary have been featured by BBC World News, MSNBC, ABC News, HuffPost, Yahoo News, and The Liberal Redneck Podcast with Trey Crowder. Havoc's poetry has appeared in *The Painted*

Cave Literary Journal ("Paradox," 2017), White Squirrel Literary Journal, *and Discarded: A Rural Anthology* (Backwoods Literary Press, 2024). Raised on old-time and bluegrass music and forged in the fire of Rage Against the Machine, she believes words should bruise, provoke, and, when necessary, howl.

Born and raised in Mount Pleasant, Texas, **Ja'Quacy Kieron Minter** is a poet, performer, and bestselling author. His debut chapbook, *Anger With No Casket Is A Haunting*, became a #1 New Release in Young Boys' and Men's Issues, and his work was featured in the 2025 Elder exhibition at the Fenix Art Gallery. A 2022 Everett Holle Award recipient from the University of Alabama, Minter writes poetry and prose that explore Borderline Personality Disorder, grief, and identity through intimate performance and page.

Lucas Evelyn Poynter grew up in Rockcastle County Kentucky, but ran away to the Golden State as a teenager. He's a poet pretending to be a plumber, and moonlights once a week as a deejay at KXSF San Francisco Community Radio.

Emily Crenshaw is a writer, artist, and lifelong tomato enthusiast from rural Georgia. Much of her recent work explores themes of nostalgia, girlhood, rage, and whimsy. In her free time, she can be found dilly-dallying with her rescue beagle or being terrorized by her sixteen-pound cat.

Alicia Wright is an Appalachian writer. She holds an MFA from Bowling Green State University and is the Editor-in-Chief of *Pictura Journal.* Her work has appeared in *Antiphony Journal, The Inflectionist Review, Does It Have Pockets, New Feathers Anthology,* and elsewhere. Her first collection of poems will be published by Pulley Press in 2026. She currently resides in West Virginia.

Flossie Hedges is a writer, visual artist, and teacher living in the mountains of southeastern Kentucky. She works at a small college that serves the Appalachian region.

Mecca Collins is a 22-year-old African American born and raised in Wheeling, West Virginia. With a passion for creativity and community, Mecca strives to make a positive impact through their words and in any other way they can.

Amy Le Ann Richardson is a writer and educator based in Carter County, Kentucky, where she lives on her family farm. She is the author of three poetry collections, including *Out of Places* (Pine Row Press, 2025), and her work has appeared in multiple journals. Amy holds an MFA from Spalding University and has received grants from the Kentucky Foundation for Women to support her writing, foodways storytelling, and environmental advocacy.

Emily M. Goldsmith (they/them) is a queer Louisiana Creole poet and writer originally from South Louisiana where they currently teach English as an Instructor at LSU. Emily received their PhD in English and Creative Writing from the University of Southern Mississippi and an MFA from the University of Kentucky. Their creative work can be found in or forthcoming from *Pithead Chapel, Midway Journal, Moist Poetry Journal, Zaum,* and elsewhere.

Marjorie Maddox, Commonwealth University Professor Emerita of English, lives in Central PA. Author of 17 poetry collections—including *Small Earthly Space* and *Seeing Things*—she has also published a story collection, four children's books, and co-edited *Common Wealth* and *Keystone Poetry* (PSU Press). She is assistant editor of *Presence* and host of WPSU-FM's *Poetry Moment*. Her forthcoming books are *Hover Here* (poetry) and *A Man Named Branch: The True Story of Baseball's Great Experiment* (middle-grade biography). Her website is www.marjoriemaddox.com.

Emma Bryan is a public historian, gardener, and writer from Central Kentucky. Their work is rooted in relationship and community building, storytelling, and critically studying the cultural history of Kentucky and the Ohio Valley. You can find Emma somewhere in the woods, reading a book, tending their garden, crafting, or walking their dogs.

Jan Wiezorek (he/him) writes from rural Michigan and is author of the poetry chapbook *Prayer's Prairie* (Michigan Writers Cooperative Press) and the forthcoming chapbook *Forests of Woundedness* (Seven Kitchens Press). He has lived in Iowa, Minnesota, Nebraska, Illinois, and now Michigan, both in small communities and in large cities.

Marianne Worthington is author of the prize-winning poetry collection, *The Girl Singer*, and a forthcoming second collection from Belle Point Press in 2026. She grew up in East Tennessee and lives, writes, and teaches in southeastern Kentucky.

Chelsey Reid is a writer and public health professional from Louisville, Kentucky, who is dedicated to dismantling systemic health disparities. She currently calls Frankfort, Kentucky, home and spends as much time as possible outdoors with her dogs.

Eric Creech is a queer poet and actor from Harlan County. He works in mental health in the Appalachia coal fields and is a member of Higher Ground. Eric was raised at the foot of Black Mountain, Kentucky's highest peak.

Olivia Dudding-Rodriguez is an Appalachian poet, storyteller, facilitator, and devoted celebrant who has made her home in Eastern Utah. Born and raised in southeastern Ohio, her work centers the stories, identities, and inheritances of rural places. Her first chapbook, *Honey Wonder*, arrived July 2024 from Moon in the Rye Press. She is the poet laureate of Helper, Utah.

Eric Morris is a writer and teacher from Morehead, KY, who currently teaches at Morehead State University and explores the intersections between language, writing, and culture in environments we create for ourselves and others. Some of his ramblings can be found at ericmorriswriter.com

Himothy Hazardus is a female-to-male transgender Appalachian drag king and community organizer from Hazard, KY. For over a decade he has performed in drag shows across the Commonwealth, most often to benefit charities on behalf of the Imperial Court of Kentucky. As a result of his pentecostal upbringing, he volunteers with several atheist organizations and works in research administration by day.

Jessica Powers is a poet and bookseller from rural Illinois. Her work has appeared in Hair Trigger, Ransack

Press, and Mulberry Literary. She is currently a graduate student pursuing a Master's in Teaching and hopes to be a High School English teacher one day. In her free time, she enjoys volunteering for conservation organizations that are working to restore Illinois prairie land.

Marianne Peel is nurturing her own creative spirit after teaching middle and high school English for thirty-two years. She lives in Lexington, KY, and can frequently be found indulging in Panera unlimited sip club as she sits across from her partner, writing together. She is passionate about words, music, playing flute, singing in gazebos, forest bathing, and learning to play the ukulele.

Beth Wolfe (she/her) is a higher education administrator and writer living in West Virginia. A native Appalachian, her work has appeared in the Women of Appalachia Project, Beltway Poetry Quarterly, and Untelling. Her house is filled with jazz and dog hair, thanks to her husband and Golden Retrievers, respectively.

Josh May (1988-2023) was a writer, producer, banjo picker, and a grinner from Magoffin County, Kentucky. He co-founded the Kentucky Rural-Urban Exchange and made important contributions to the Appalachian region through his work at Appalshop, the Appalachian Media Institute, the Highlander Center, the Media Action Grassroots Network, South Magoffin Community Activists, and the Stay Together Appalachian Youth Project. He also made a big mark on Kentucky's punk and traditional music scenes as the head of the DIY record label Karmic Swamp, a producer for June Appal Recordings, and a founding member of the worker-owned cooperative Roundabout Music Company. Josh was a tenth-generation Kentuckian and loved to make people feel welcome and like they belonged in Eastern Kentucky. The enclosed poems were originally published by the Governor's School for the Arts as a chapbook entitled "Shed Like Snake Hide."

Kelli Claypool White is an Administrative Assistant living in Lexington, Kentucky. She writes of her experiences and of the larger impact on her children's lives.

Cassidy White is a lawyer and policy strategist from rural western Kentucky. She is the National Public Health Policy Lead at The Council of State Governments, where she works with all three branches of government to bolster health outcomes across the nation (and is fortunate to do so in her beloved Louisville). Cassidy is an avid reader and writer—in both work and play—and revels in finding and forming community through storytelling.

Jovan Mays is a poet, teacher, wrestling coach, and justice advocate from Aurora, CO. His work hinges on the Chinua Achebe quote, "Until the lions have their own historians, history of the hunt will always glorify the hunter." Mays strives to write for the lions. He is the inaugural and emeritus Poet Laureate of Aurora, Colorado, a National Poetry Slam Champion, and TED speaker.

Trecinda Wilder (she/her) is a Biloxi-born author whose works reflect the experiences of Southern women fighting for survival under a racist, misogynist, fundamentalist patriarchy. Drawing from the cultural stigmas and strengths originating with the donors of her own colorful DNA, Wilder uses Southern Gothic style to bring a voice to those who have been denied one.

Cassandra Ruby is from Caldwell, Idaho. She has overcome domestic violence, addiction, and systematic oppression. She is a mother, a survivor, and a poet.

Bradley Firchow lives in Eastern Kentucky, where the hills, hollers, and people who call them home shape his work. He co-founded the CATS Clinic, a student-run clinic bringing free care to Morehead, Kentucky. A member of the Sawstone Writers Guild and the Kentucky Storytelling Community of Practice, he believes stories can move us toward health for Appalachian land and people.

Lexie Stepro's destiny is to alchemize her pain into language, or at least that's what her astrology app says. After temporarily moving back to her hometown of LaGrange, KY, she's working to reclaim old bus routes, smoke spots, and the starry night sky.

Kelsey Voit is a queer farmer and food justice organizer based in Louisville, Kentucky. With observant childlike wonder, they weave threads of nature and selfhood into poetry and folk music. Their work has previously been published in samfiftyfour.

Jude DeWalt is a trans poet and student haunting Western Pennsylvania, where Appalachia and the Great Lakes overlap.

Leo Coffey is a queer writer born and raised in western North Carolina. His creative work focuses on themes of memory, rural life, and LGBTQ+ narratives. His work has appeared in The Appalachian Review, The Dead Mule School of Southern Literature, and Salvation South. He is currently pursuing his MFA at the University of Kentucky.

Ceirra Evans is a Kentucky (US)–based painter depicting Appalachia and rural narratives. Her work has been reviewed by *Hyperallergic*, *The New Yorker*, and other publications, and has been exhibited in 21c Museums in Louisville, Kentucky, and Bentonville, Arkansas. She has presented the solo exhibitions "Come Home With Me" at Virginia Tech's Perspective Gallery (Blacksburg, VA), "A Wild Weed" at Gallerie Geraldine Banier (Paris, France), and "Be Careful Out There" at Moremen Gallery (Louisville, KY). Her most recent show, "Come Rain or Shine," was held at Institute 193 (Lexington, KY).

9 798218 942885